Creative Writing Booklets:

EASY TO MAKE—EASY TO USE

by Flora Joy

illustrated by Pat Harroll and Flora Joy

Cover by Vanessa Filkins

Copyright © Good Apple, Inc., 1985

GOOD APPLE, INC.
BOX 299
CARTHAGE, IL 62321

Dedicated to Henry

Copyright © Good Apple, Inc., 1985

ISBN No. 0-86653-274-9

Printing No. 7654

GOOD APPLE, INC.
BOX 299
CARTHAGE, IL 62321-0299

The purchase of this book entitles the buyer to reproduce student activity pages for classroom use only. Any other use requires written permission from Good Apple, Inc.

How to Use This Book

This book consists of 27 Creative Writing Booklets for motivating students from preschool through the middle grades to practice and develop the skills of creative expression (either written or oral) in addition to other specific language skills.

The following is provided for each Creative Writing Booklet: a full-page design, a half-page design, and student or instructor information cards.

Student/Instructor Cards

These cards generally center around the following areas:

A. *Story Starters* which may be read to or given to the students for them to complete—either orally or in writing.

B. *Story Situations* which may be used in the same fashion as Story Starters.

C. *Language Study* information which would generally be used by the instructor for discussion and specific language skill development. In addition to all the communication skills developed with creative writing or creative oral expression experiences, the global areas of language skills which are most frequently suggested with the use of these *Story Shapes* are the *Comprehension* of selected *Expressions, Homographs,* and *Homophones.*

Comprehension of selected expressions may be discussed as they appear on the provided captions. Examples of those included in this book are "Things That Bowl Me Over" or "Keep This Under Your Hat." In all cases the meaning of the expression appears on the Language Study Card.

Interpretation of homophones may be taught through these shapes. Homophones are words which have identical sounds but different spellings and meanings. Some examples of homophones included in captions are "Tense Times" or "Things DEAR to Me." In all cases the meanings and spellings of these homophones are provided on the Language Study Cards.

Interpretation of homographs may also be taught through these shapes. Homographs are words with the same spelling, but with different meanings or origins. Some examples included in captions are "Things I Can't BEAR" or "Things That BUG Me."

The concept of "Writing Therapy" may be used with these shapes. Writing therapy refers to the technique of allowing students to write as a means of releasing tension, stress, or frustrations. Some captions selected for this purpose are "Things That Drive Me NUTS" or "Things That BURN Me Up."

The "Tall Tale" may also be encouraged through selected story shapes. "A Ghost Story," "A DOGgone Good Story," or "A Corny Story" are sample stimuli for this category.

Table of Contents

How to Use This Book
TURTLE: The Race
FIRE: Things That BURN Me Up!
TENT: Tense Times
BEAR: Things I Can't BEAR
GHOST: A Ghost Story
ACORN: Things That Drive Me NUTS!
SCISSORS: Cut It Out!
DEER: Things DEAR to Me
BRUSH: The Brush-Off
HARP: Things My Mother HARPS on Too Much
16: When I'm 16
LIGHT SWITCH: Things That Turn Me Off
CLOCK: Good Times
BUG: Things That BUG Me
BANANA: An ApPEALing Tale
BOXING GLOVE: Things I'd Fight For
MATCH: The Perfect Match
BOWLING PINS: Things That BOWL Me Over
CHEST: My Treasures
HAT: Keep This Under Your Hat
FAN: A FANtastic Person
DINOSAUR: Things I Wish Were Extinct
2: It Hurts TOO Much
DOG: A DOGgone Good Story
NO
CORN: A Corny Story
BALLOON: An Uplifting Experience

Many additional language skills may be developed both with the provided captions and those suggested as caption substitutions.

D. *Caption Substitutions* which may be used *instead* of the one which appears on each design. These captions may be written or typed, then pasted over the original caption. Different story starters, situations, and language skills may be used with these new captions.

E. *Decorative Possibilities* which may enhance the flat paper design.

Design Preparation

All designs, which may either be removed from the text or photocopied onto other types/colors of paper, may be used in a variety of different visual formats. If designs are photocopied, consider copying onto various colors of ditto paper, construction paper, fluorescent paper, or other brands/names of special papers/colors. Designs may also be traced or drawn onto various papers. For final preparation for student use, consider the following suggestions:

Preparation of Larger Design

1. Photocopy or remove larger design from text, then staple atop several blank pages of the same size. Have students write their story/responses onto these blank pages.

2. Follow Step 1, but place staple(s) inside design area near top or upper left corner. Cut through all pages at once for a shape booklet.

3. Photocopy or remove larger design from text, then prepare as a Task Card. Selected student information sections may be pasted on the backs. For added permanency, consider covering with a protective clear film, such as laminating paper.

Front of Task Card:

Back of Task Card:

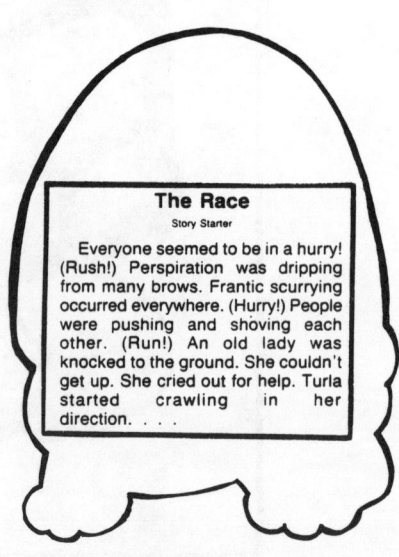

4. Photocopy or remove larger design from text, then trim at outside border. Paste onto a file folder or small backdrop to be used as a learning center. Prepare provided student information cards and add others appropriate for participating learners. Those using center may select desired tasks.

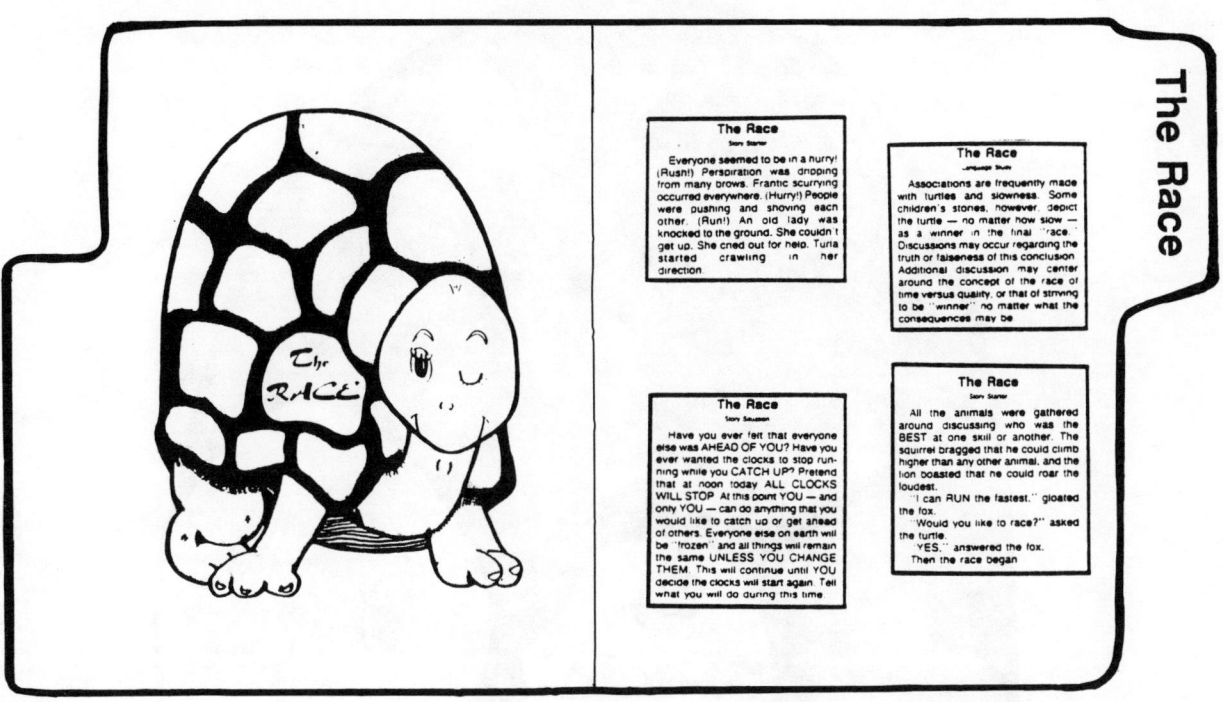

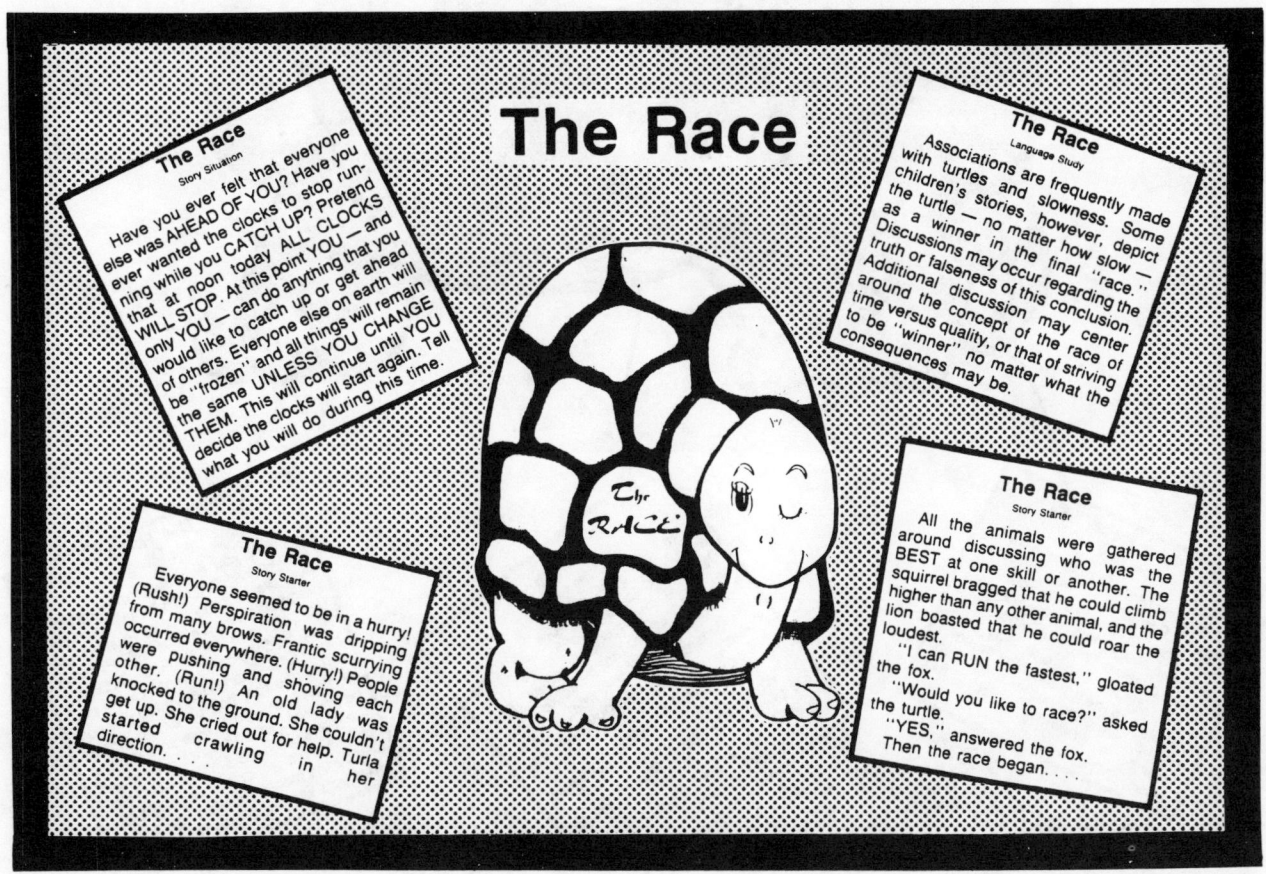

5. Prepare a mobile by photocopying or removing larger design from text. Selected student task sections may be prepared as miniature task cards, then appended with cord, rubber bands, or paper clips.

Preparation of Even Larger Design

6. Using an opaque or overhead projector, enlarge design to poster board or bulletin board size. Place design in center of board and display students' written responses around the design.

A multitude of additional uses may be made of these designs. Please feel free to experiment and create many other exciting language experiences for your students. Above all, use your imagination and have fun!

Preparation of Smaller Design

7. Photocopy or remove page with smaller design from the text, then fold the sheet at the center of the page. Prepare booklets by adding desired number of blank pages of the same size. In this fashion the design will appear on the "cover" with the student information on the back. Note that any portions of the student/instructor information which you prefer to be omitted may be covered prior to photocopying. If *all* information appears, students may be given directions regarding *which* one(s) to use—*or* they may select the one of their choice.

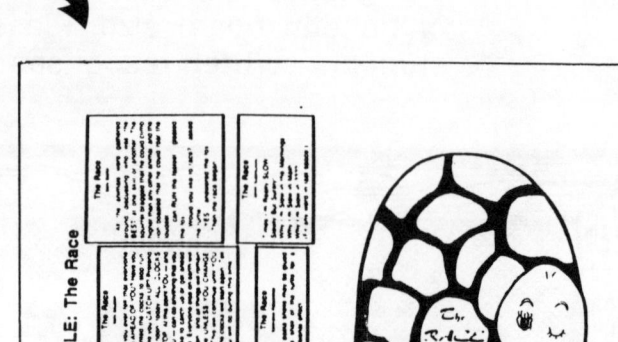
(Photocopy of page)

(Two—five blank pages)

(All sheets placed together, stapled at center, then folded)

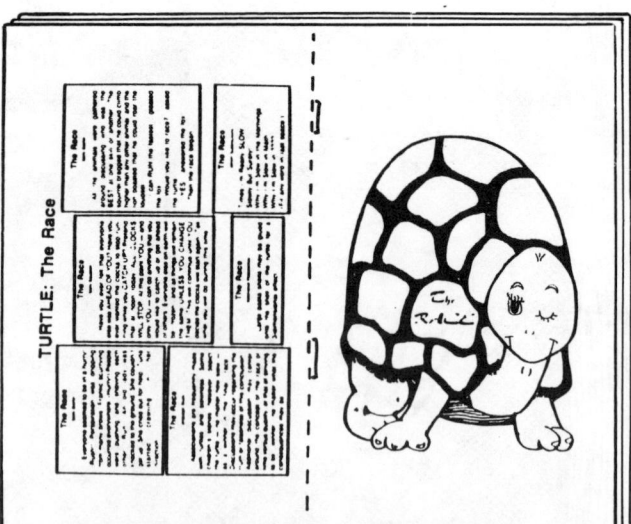

(Creative writing booklet ready for student use)

8. By following any of the suggestions for the larger designs, booklets, shapes, or task cards may be prepared half size. This smaller size sometimes has greater appeal for the older students than does the larger size.

TURTLE: The Race

The Race
Story Starter

Everyone seemed to be in a hurry! (Rush!) Perspiration was dripping from many brows. Frantic scurrying occurred everywhere. (Hurry!) People were pushing and shoving each other. (Run!) An old lady was knocked to the ground. She couldn't get up. She cried out for help. Turla started crawling in her direction....

The Race
Language Study

Associations are frequently made with turtles and slowness. Some children's stories, however, depict the turtle—no matter how slow—as a winner in the final "race." Discussions may occur regarding the truth or falseness of this conclusion. Additional discussion may center around the concept of the race of time versus quality, or that of striving to be "winner" no matter what the consequences may be.

The Race
Story Situation

Have you ever felt that everyone else was ahead of you? Have you ever wanted the clocks to stop running while you caught up? Pretend that at noon today all clocks will stop. At this point *you*—and only *you*—can do anything that you would like to catch up or get ahead of others. Everyone else on earth will be "frozen" and all things will remain the same *unless* you change them. This will continue until *you* decide the clocks will start again. Tell what you will do during this time.

The Race
Decorative Possibilities

Large pasta shells may be glued onto the shell of the turtle for a 3-dimensional effect.

The Race
Story Starter

All the animals were gathered around discussing who was the *best* at one skill or another. The squirrel bragged that he could climb higher than any other animal, and the lion boasted that he could roar the loudest.

"I can *run* the fastest," gloated the fox.

"Would you like to race?" asked the turtle.

"Yes," answered the fox.

Then the race began....

The Race
Caption Substitutions

Times I'm Really Slow
Slowly But Surely!
Why I'm Slow in the Mornings
Why I'm Slow in Math
Why I'm Slow in ????
(Fit any word in last space.)

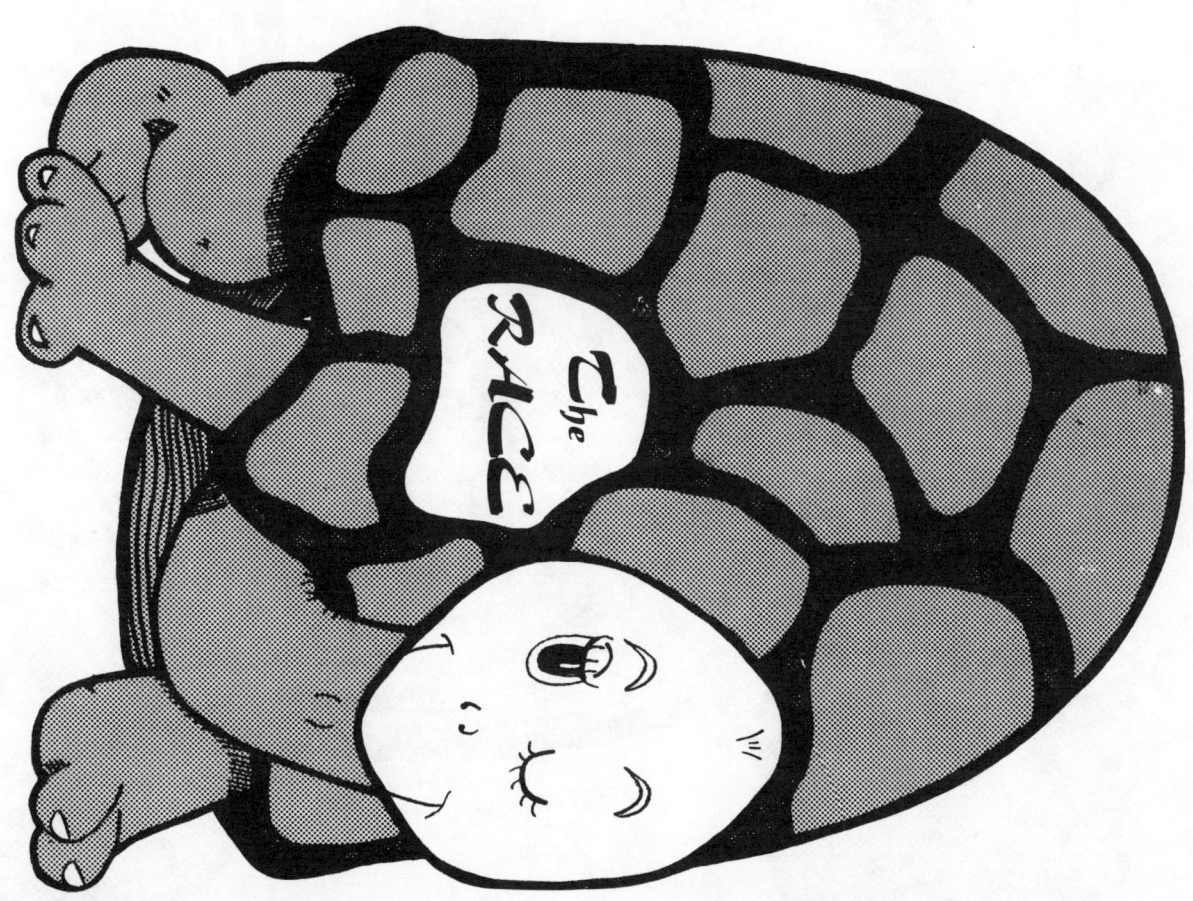

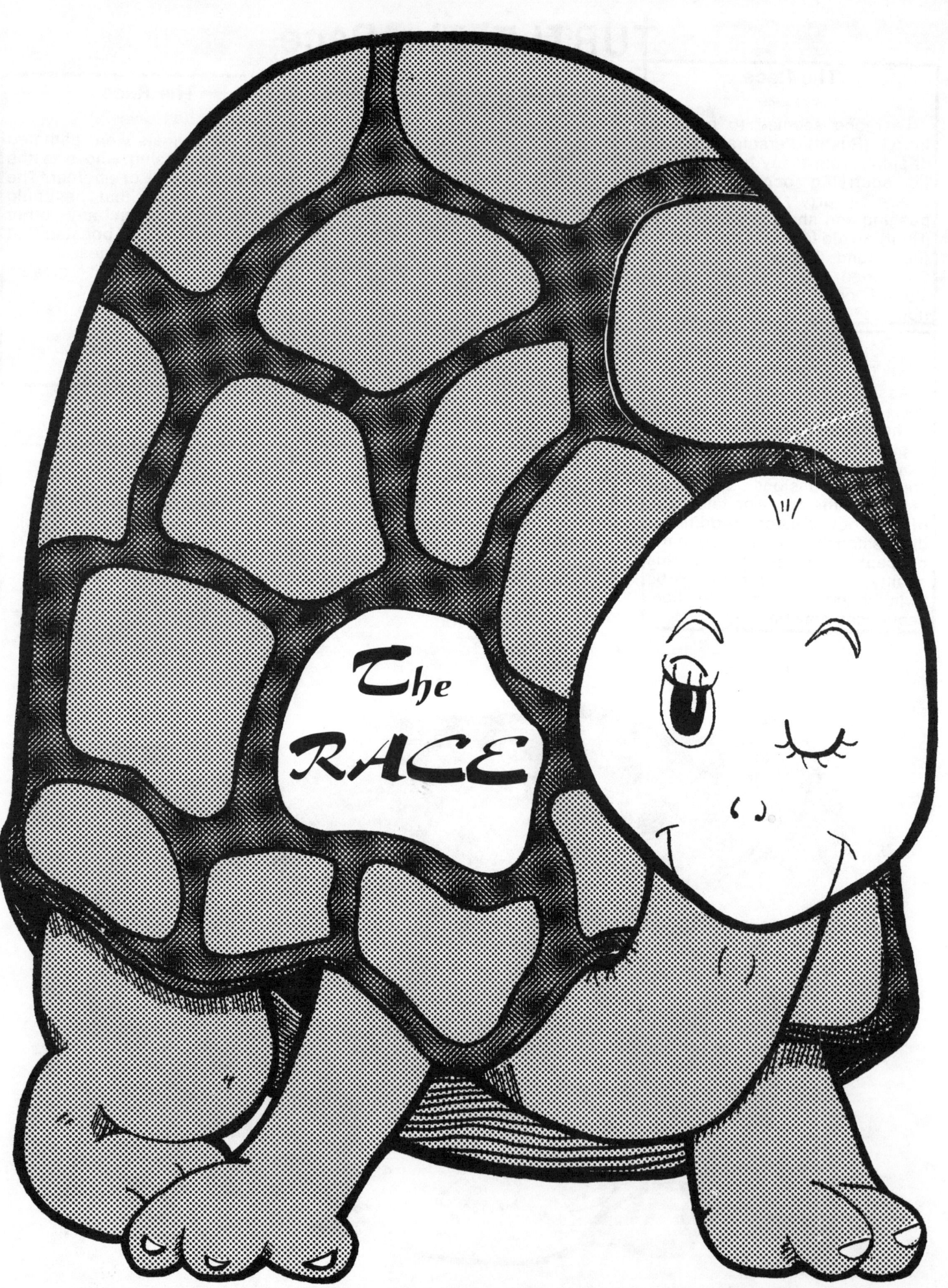

FIRE: Things That BURN Me Up!

Things That BURN Me Up!
Story Situation

What makes you angry? Think about things that have happened recently that have been upsetting to you. What can quickly trigger a "maddening" response in you? Select one instance that has made you angry (or would "burn you up") and describe the experience in detail. Tell *why* you became angry. Try to determine the *reason* for your anger. Also consider how you would be able to *control* your feelings if a similar occurrence happened in the future.

Things That BURN Me Up!
Caption Substitutions

A Burning Experience
Things I Get Fired Up Over
People Who Light My Fire
A Warm Winter's Tale
By the Fireplace
A Cure for Burnout

Things That BURN Me Up!
Language Study

How do you think the expression "burn me up" originated? Do we really *burn up* when we become angry? Explain your answer. If we do not literally *burn up*, then why do you think we use these actual words? What is the difference in this expression and one using "burning up" when the temperature is too high? (Words such as *burn* are called homographs. Homographs are words which are spelled the same but have different meanings. Other common examples of homographs are *run, bank,* or *fly.*)

Think of other expressions we may use to describe our anger, such as "that makes my blood boil." What are the literal and figurative meanings of these expressions? Are there homographs in any of these expressions? If so, what are they and what are their different meanings?

Things That BURN Me Up!
Story Starter

The sultry siren slowly pushed open the door leading into my room. Her silent stare sent chills over my body. Her eyes flickered both with evil and delight. Then I realized what she was planning. My chills changed to flames. She had done this many times before and had always gone unpunished. I had to stop her, but I knew of only one way. I must move quickly . . . .

Things That BURN Me Up!
Decorative Possibilities

Yellow tissues may be glued onto the flame design for a 3-dimensional effect. Wood-grain self-adhesive decorative paper may be pasted over the log area of the design. Also, real wood chips, bark chips, or sticks may be glued onto the log area of the design.

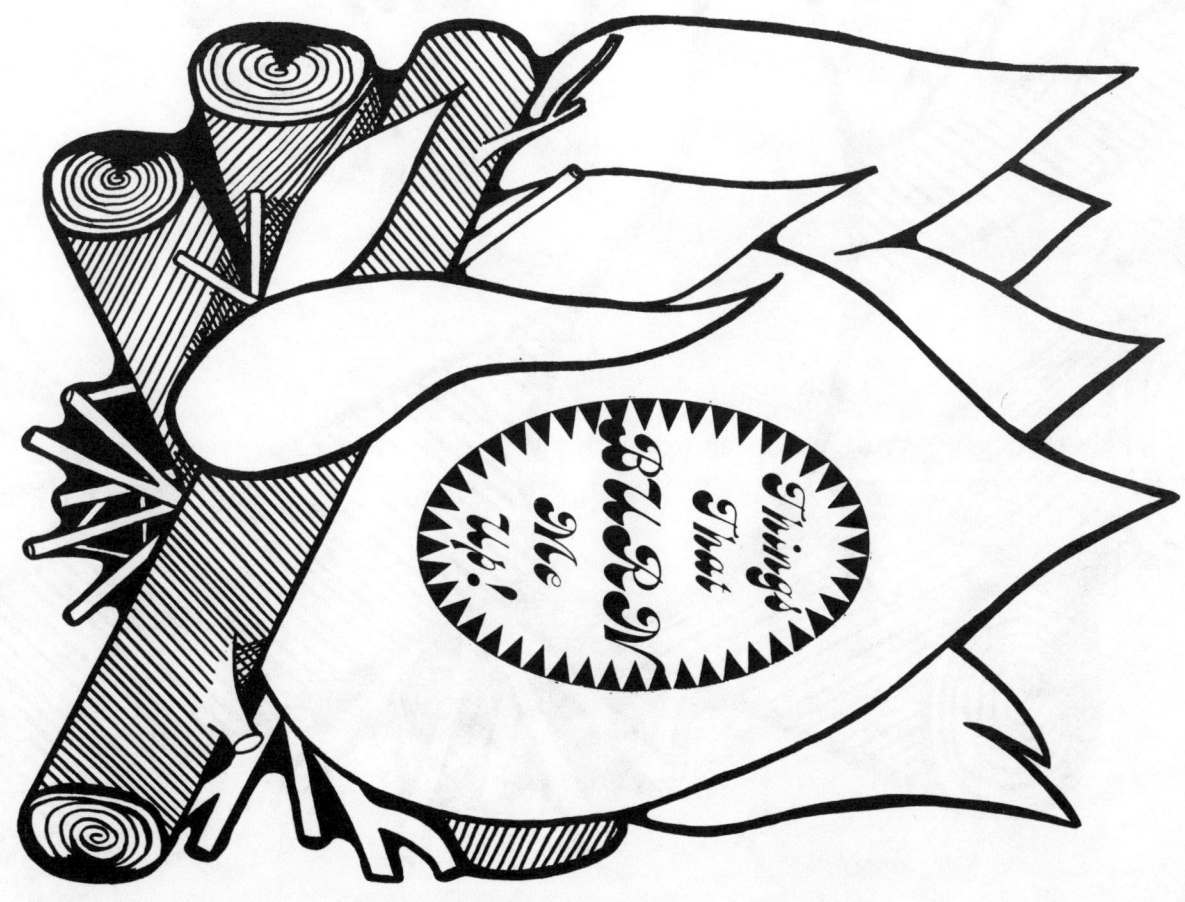

TENT: Tense Times

Tense Times
Story Starter
Our vacation was certainly different this year. There were no snakes in the tent like last year; there were no bears in the park like the previous year; and the weather was quite pleasant unlike many other vacation periods. However, this year . . . .

Tense Times
Story Starter
The sink was stacked with dishes. For three days they had not been washed. The baby was screaming. Did he want food or attention? Toys were scattered throughout the house. The faucet had broken and water had already begun to fill the basement. A storm threatened. The doorbell rang. As I headed for the front door, the telephone rang. Now what?!?!?. . . .

Tense Times
Language Study
Words which sound the same but have different spellings and meanings are called homophones. The words *tents* and *tense* are examples. *Tense* means not relaxed or showing strain. *Tents* means more than one tent.

Tense Times
Caption Substitutions
Pay AtTENTion to . . .
A Camping Trip I'll Never Forget
How to Relieve Tension
A TENTative Solution

Tense Times
Decorative Possibilities
Real canvas or brown felt may be glued onto the tent shape cut from cardboard. Wire, such as that from a coat hanger, may add special effects to the design.

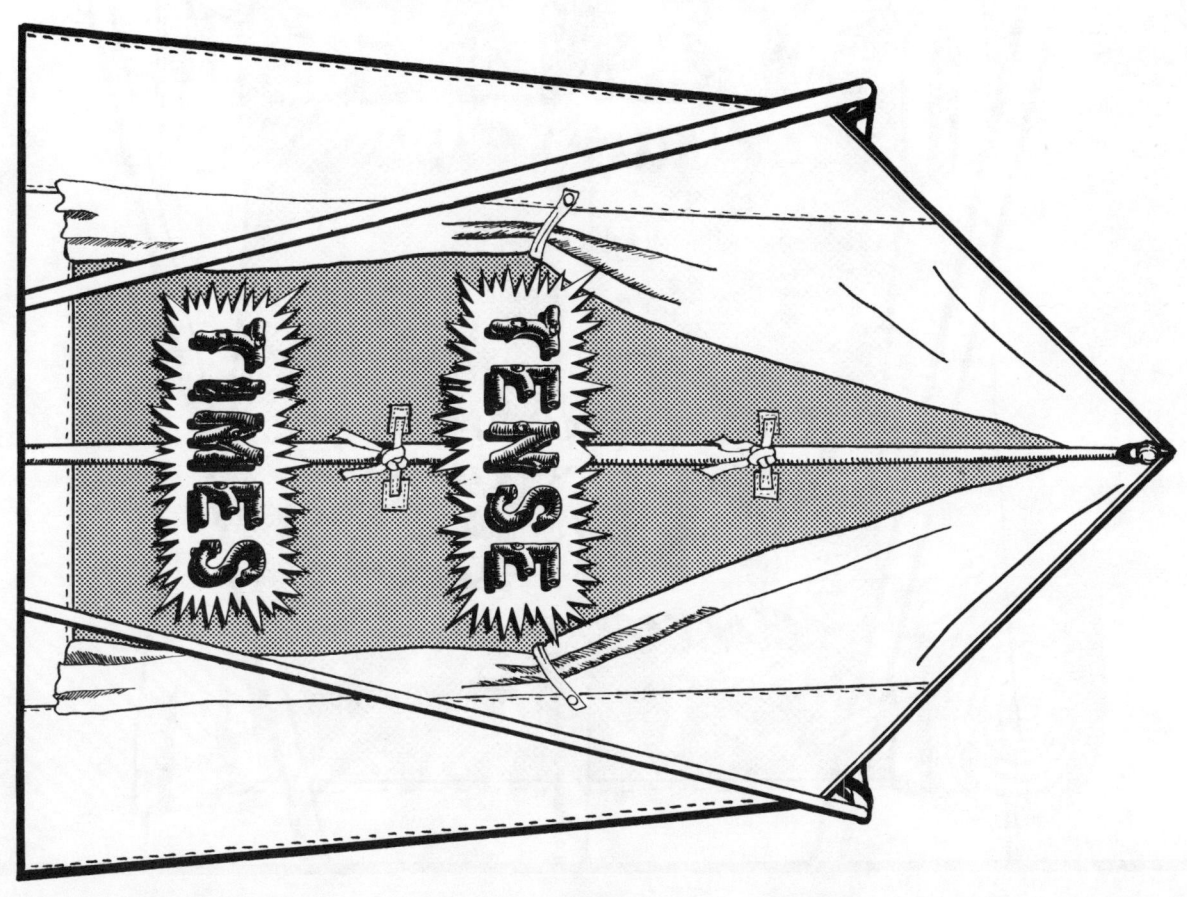

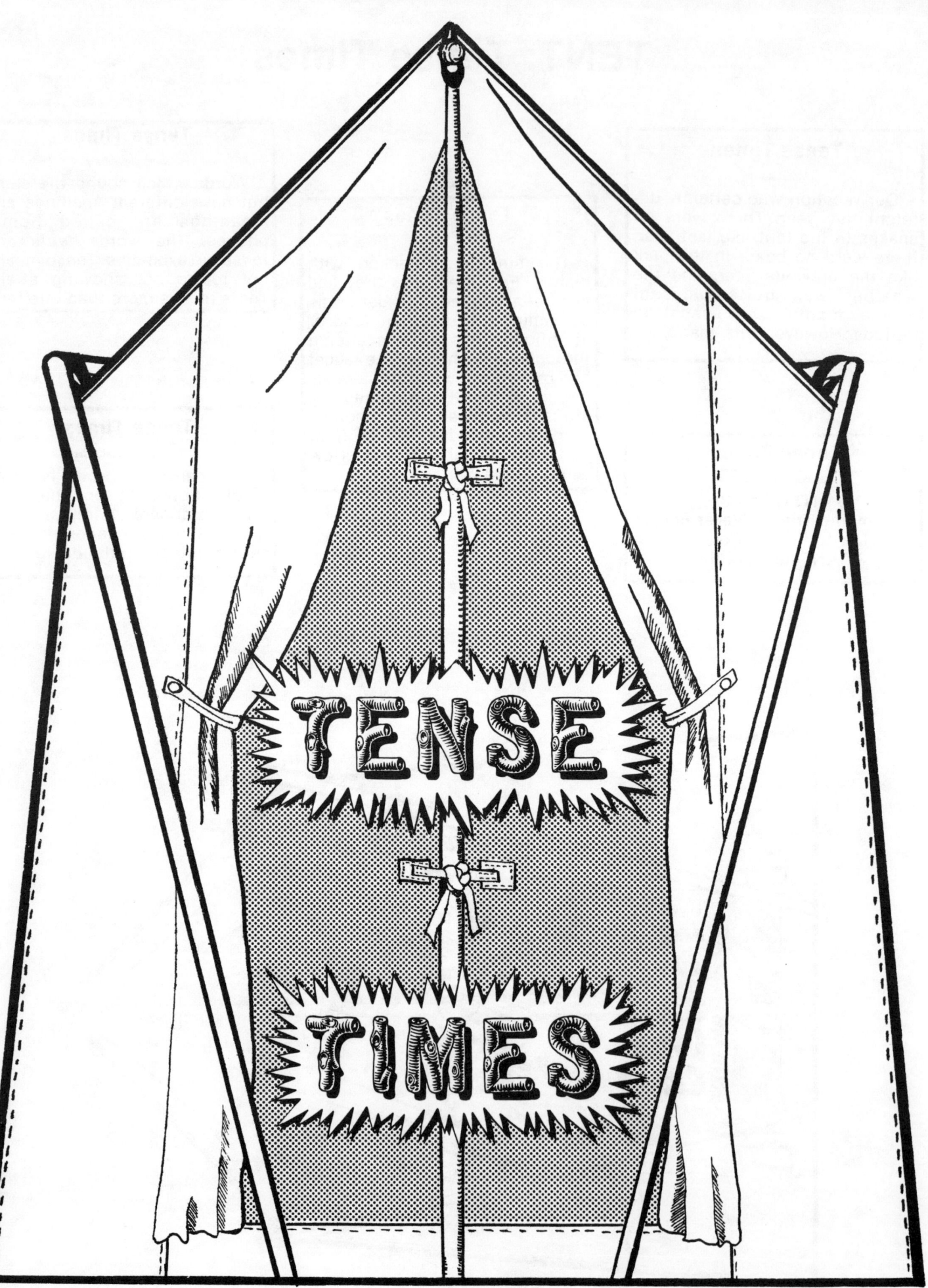

BEAR: Things I Can't BEAR

Things I Can't BEAR
Story Situation

Tomorrow is this bear's birthday. Your "present" to him is a promise to eliminate three habits which *you* have that are unbearable to others. Tell what these three habits are and explain how you plan to eliminate them.

Things I Can't BEAR
Caption Substitutions

The BEAR Facts
How to Give a BEAR Hug
A Time I BARELy Escaped
The BARE Necessities of Life
The BEARfoot Beast

Things I Can't BEAR
Story Situation

Think of some things that you feel you just can't bear—or things you would really hate to see happen. Make a list of the things you feel would be the *most difficult* to bear—putting at the top of the list the things you would *most* hate to have happen. Then select *one* of these items you have listed and describe how you think the occurrence can be *prevented*.

Things I Can't BEAR
Language Study

The expression "things I can't bear" is used to refer to situations that generally cannot be endured. In this expression the word *bear* is a homograph. Homographs are words which are spelled the same but have different meanings. Think of other expressions which we use to refer to things we cannot endure.

Things I Can't BEAR
Decorative Possibilities

A fur, fake-fur, or brown velveteen fabric may be glued onto the bear-shaped design. Atop this fabric, craft moveable eyes may be glued.

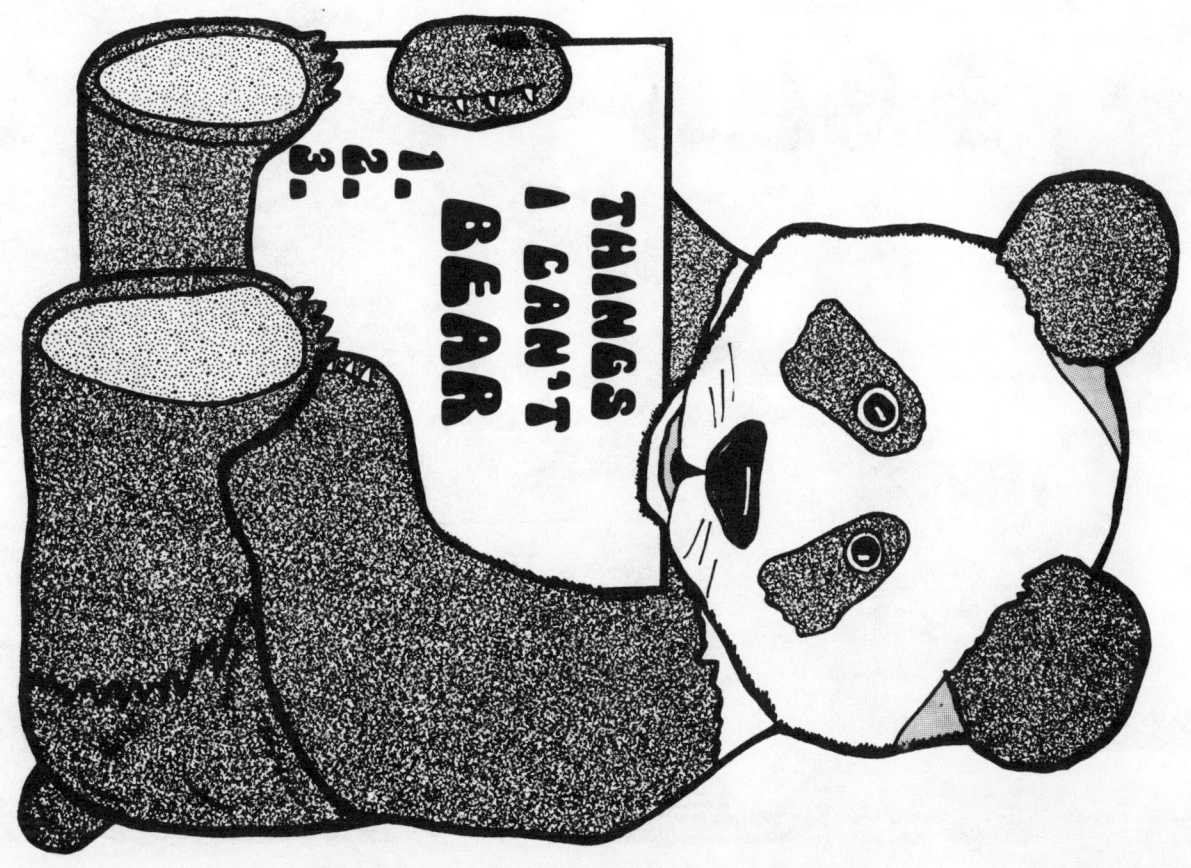

GHOST: A Ghost Story

A Ghost Story
Story Starter

"Something is outside our tent," whispered Mike to his younger brother. Jimmy rolled over in his sleeping bag.

"I don't hear anything," Jimmy mumbled.

A faint pale glow began to appear through the nearby brush.

"Look," Mike choked.

Both boys peered through the canvas opening . . . .

A Ghost Story
Caption Substitutions

The Night I Was
Scared out of My Wits
The Haunted House
The Strange Spectre
The Time I Didn't Have
A Ghost of a Chance
The Time I Wished I Could Be Invisible
The Ghost of My Dreams
The Scariest Thing I've Ever Seen

A Ghost Story
Story Starter

The Ghostville Glooms began their annual meeting. An excitement filled the air. It was time for the selection of new members. Any ghost who wanted to join must have scared the wits out of a human during the past year. The five who had done the best job were selected as new members of the club. Each ghost told its story as the old members listened.

"Gregg Ghost will be first," announced the club president.

"O-o-o-o-oh, well," began Gregg, "I . . . .

A Ghost Story
Story Starter

Mr. Lee's car rolled to a dead halt on Sims Road. He knew he should not have tried to take a shortcut into Ruddtown, but it was late and he wanted to get home before the storm. No sound came from the engine as he tried to start it again. A gust of wind seemed to give the car a violent thrust. Mr. Lee decided to leave the car and walk toward a small building which he could see outlined in the horizon each time lightning illuminated the skies. He opened his car door and . . . .

A Ghost Story
Decorative Possibilities

Cut a cardboard shape similar to that of the ghost design. Drape a white handkerchief or piece of white fabric over this cardboard shape. Adhere moveable eyes at the appropriate places on the design.

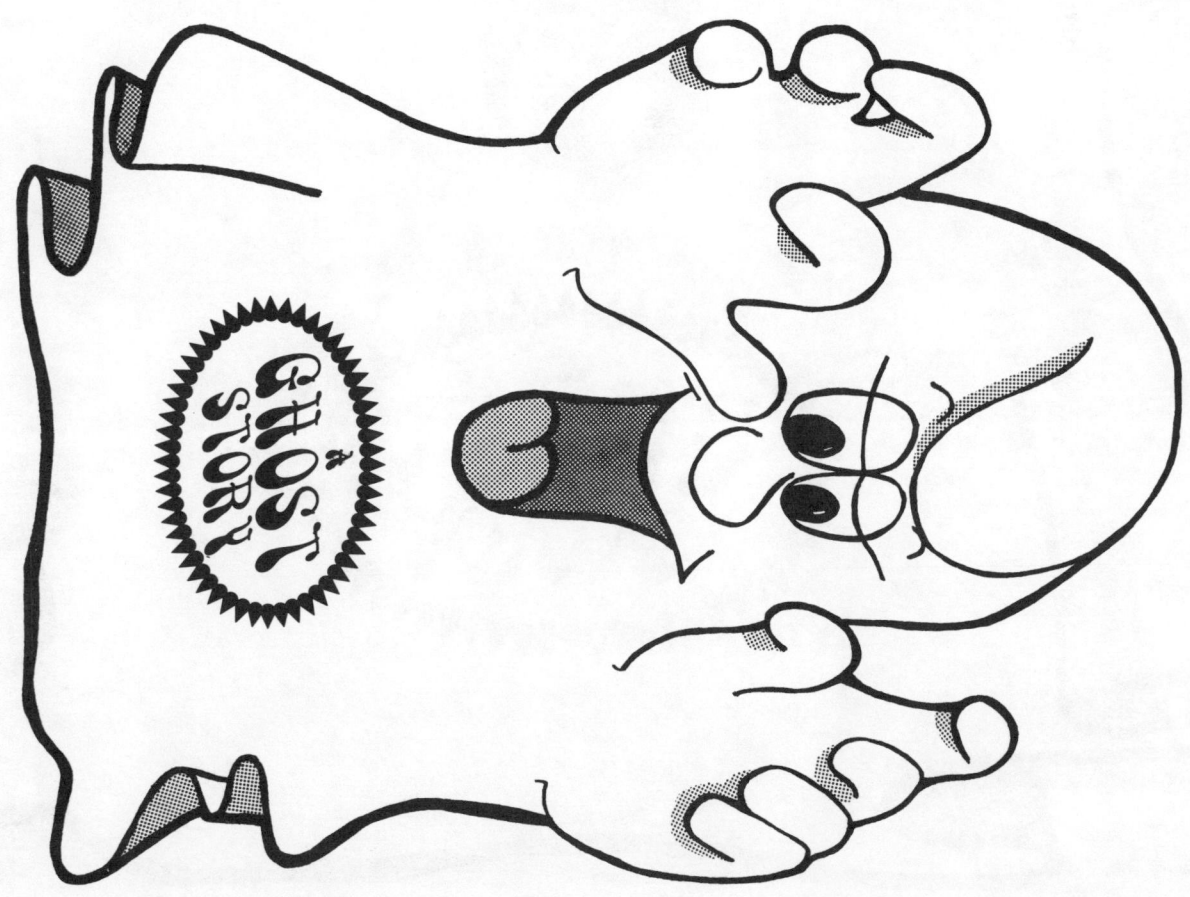

ACORN: Things That Drive Me NUTS!

Things That Drive Me NUTS!
Story Starter

The noise . . . It began almost unnoticeably. At first I didn't even mind. Then it grew louder. And louder. AND LOUDER. I thought I was going crazy. Will it ever stop? Let me tell you how it sounds and how it makes me feel . . . .

Things That Drive Me NUTS!
Story Situation

In the *Guinness Book of World Records*, Lynn Mercer should be listed as the one kid who has driven every teacher nuts. Describe three incidents which might have happened in Lynn's classroom which might have helped Lynn earn this record.

Things That Drive Me NUTS!
Language Study

The expression "drive me nuts" generally refers to actions which are extremely annoying. Make a list of other expressions which you use when the behaviors of others almost drive you crazy.

Things That Drive Me NUTS!
Caption Substitutions

A-Corny Story
I Act Nutty When . . . .
The Nuttiest Friend I Have
I'm Just Nuts Over . . . .
The Squirrel's Delight

Things That Drive Me NUTS!
Decorative Possibilities

Pieces of shells from nuts may be glued onto the basic acorn design. Selected tasks may be appended to actual nuts—with all affixed to the large design.

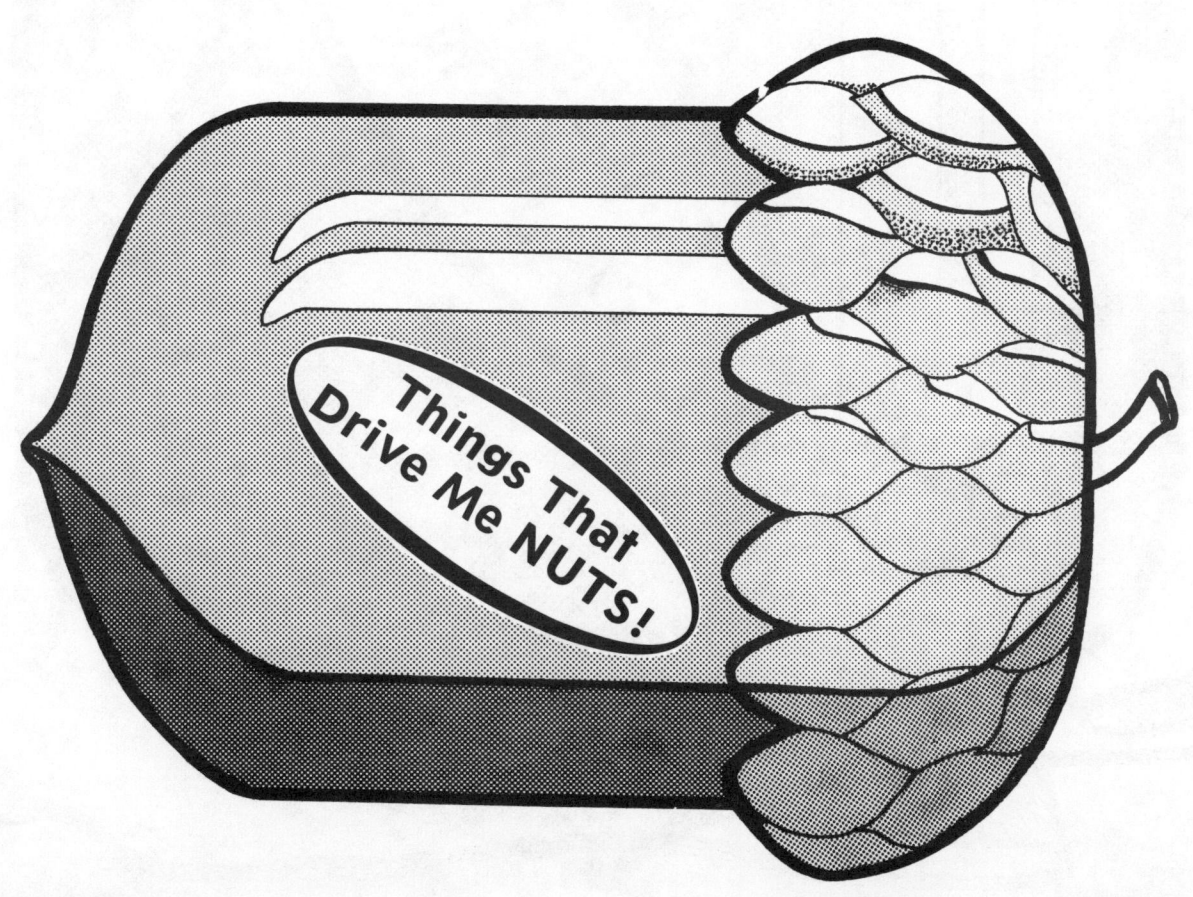

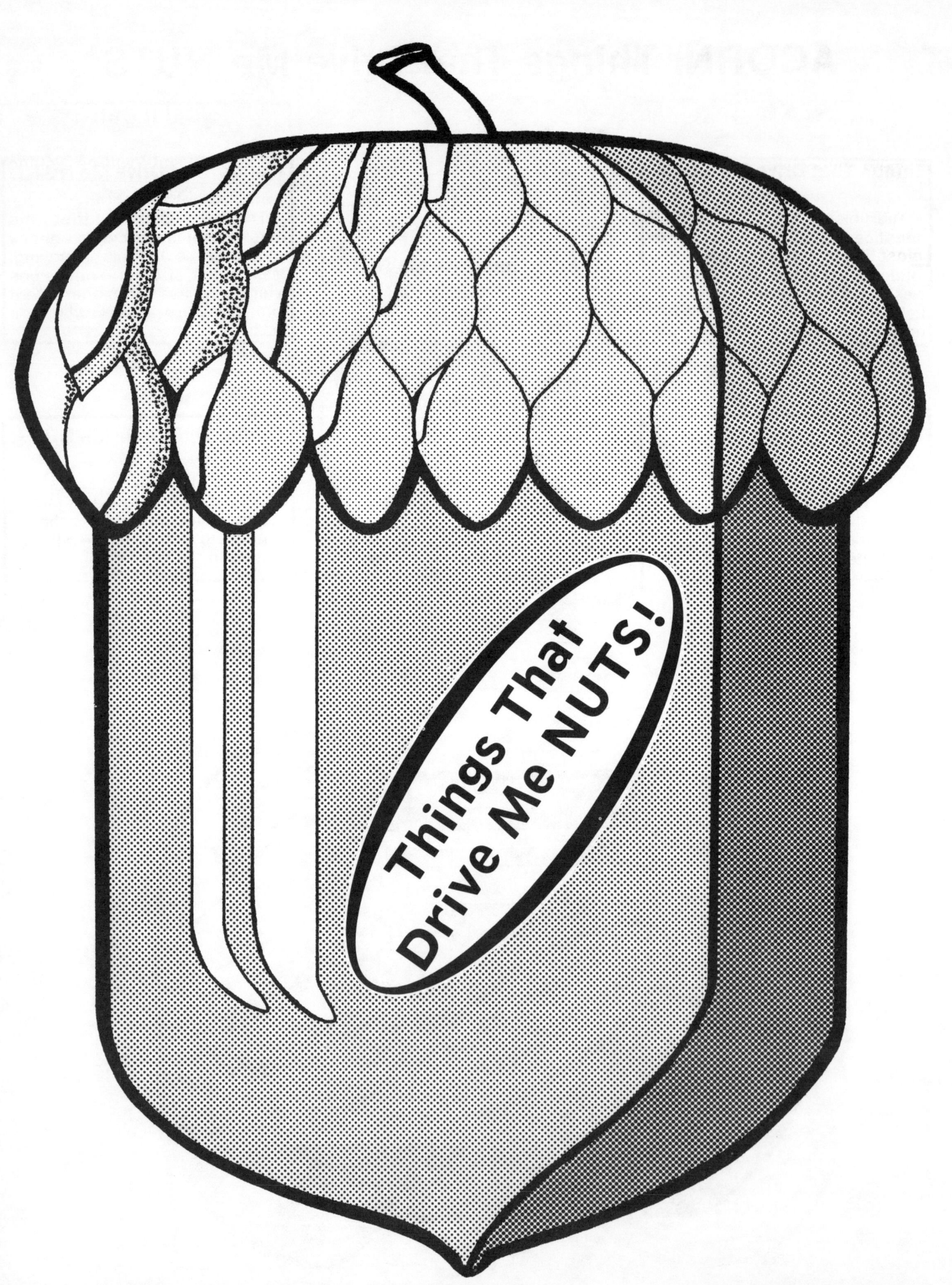

SCISSORS: Cut It Out!

Cut It Out!
Story Situation
Many things happen frequently which annoy us. Describe ten things which happen that you would like to see stopped. Place a check by the three you would *most* like to see "cut out."

Cut It Out!
Language Study
The expression "cut it out" means that one is requesting that an activity or behavior be stopped. It is not meant to be interpreted as a literal "cutting" as with scissors. Words spelled the same but used with different meanings in various contexts are called homographs. The word *cut* is used as a homograph in these contexts. Make a list of other expressions which we use for wanting something to be stopped. Are there any differences in the literal and the figurative meanings of words in these expressions? Are there any homographs used?

Cut It Out!
Story Situation
Skeeter Skunk will be visiting with you next week. At any time someone does something annoying, you may yell "Cut it out!" If that person continues to annoy you, Skeeter will then "reward" the offender with a new "perfume." Tell about one incident which you think will occur.

Cut It Out!
Decorative Possibilities
Aluminum foil or silver self-adhesive paper may be used on the appropriate parts of this design. Since some scissors have handles with color (orange or black), desired colors may be added. An alternative paper response for students may be prepared with permanent cardboard scissors to be used with paper sheets only the size of the paper shown between scissor blades.

Cut It Out!
Caption Substitutions
Times to Cut Up
A Cutting Remark
The Weapon
The Big Cutup
Sheer Nonsense

DEER: Things DEAR to Me

Things DEAR to Me
Story Starter

"You're such a DEAR," Mrs. Ellis said as she pinched my cheek and shook my entire head. "No one else in the whole neighborhood would have done this for me."

I was beginning to regret helping her. What if my friends found out? I would never hear the end of it. But Mrs. Ellis really had needed . . . .

Things DEAR to Me
Story Situation

There are many things of value to us that do not cost any money. Describe five things dear to *you* which cannot be purchased for any price.

Things DEAR to Me
Caption Substitutions

DEAR Mr. President:
DEAR Mom:
My DEAR Friend
The DEARest Gift I've Ever Received
Oh, DEAR!
I'm a Little DEAR When . . . .

Things DEAR to Me
Language Study

Words which sound the same but have different spellings and meanings are called homophones. The words DEER and DEAR are examples. DEAR means highly valued or loved. DEER means a large cud-chewing animal.

Things DEAR to Me
Decorative Possibilities

Glue fake-fur fabric onto a piece of cardboard cut in the deer shape. Antlers may be cut from manila file folders. Moveable eyes may be glued on and remaining design drawn on with felt markers.

Things DEAR to Me
Story Situation

Make a list of all the things you think would be DEAR to a DEER.

BRUSH: The Brush-Off

The Brush-Off
Story Starter
"Who's next?" asked the clerk.
"I am," I answered.
"I am," bellowed a large woman named Mrs. Smith.
"But I was here first," I offered.
"And how may I help you, Mrs. Smith?" the clerk responded briskly.
I was furious....

The Brush-Off
Story Starter
I always thought Melanie was the prettiest girl in the whole school. Her clothes were always neat and expensive looking. Her hair was always clean and shiny. Her complexion was always flawless. One day I managed to speak to her.
"You look so nice today," I stammered.
"I guess *you* would think so," she huffed.
Suddenly I felt....

The Brush-Off
Language Study
The expression "the brush-off" generally refers to a quick and sometimes rude dismissal of a suggestion or topic. How would you describe your feelings regarding being rudely dismissed when you have made a suggestion? Make a list of such expressions.

The Brush-Off
Caption Substitutions
Getting a Handle on Things
A Bristling Experience
The Brush Salesman's Story
Once I Was a Brush....
How to Brush Away the Blues

The Brush-Off
Decorative Possibilities
Yarn, threads, or fine strings of various sorts may be glued onto the bristle area of the brush. Wood-grain self-adhesive paper may be added to the handle area.

HARP: Things My Mother HARPS on Too Much

Things My Mother HARPS on Too Much
Story Starter

"Clean your room," I heard my mom yell. She has harped on me to clean up my room for months! I hear it over and over! If she isn't yelling about that, it's something else. Just during last week she has harped on at least a dozen different things. First of all she got really mad about . . . .

Things My Mother HARPS on Too Much
Caption Substitutions

That's Music to My Ears
Times When I'm an Angel
Heavenly Things

(In the provided title, the word *Mother* may be replaced with *Brother, Father, Sister,* etc.)

Things My Mother HARPS on Too Much
Decorative Possibilities

Strings, yarn, rubber bands, or thin wires may be glued onto the harp design for an added visual effect. Also, gold self-adhesive decorative paper may be adhered to the outer frame of the harp.

Things My Mother HARPS on Too Much
Story Starter

I had been home only ten minutes before I began to feel it coming. She was going to be angry again. I had tried so hard to do what she had asked. However . . . .

Things My Mother HARPS on Too Much
Language Study

The expression "harp on" does not literally mean that someone is playing a harp. It has a figurative meaning which refers to the fact that someone keeps on and on griping or complaining about something. Make a list of some other expressions which you use when someone repetitively dwells on one issue.

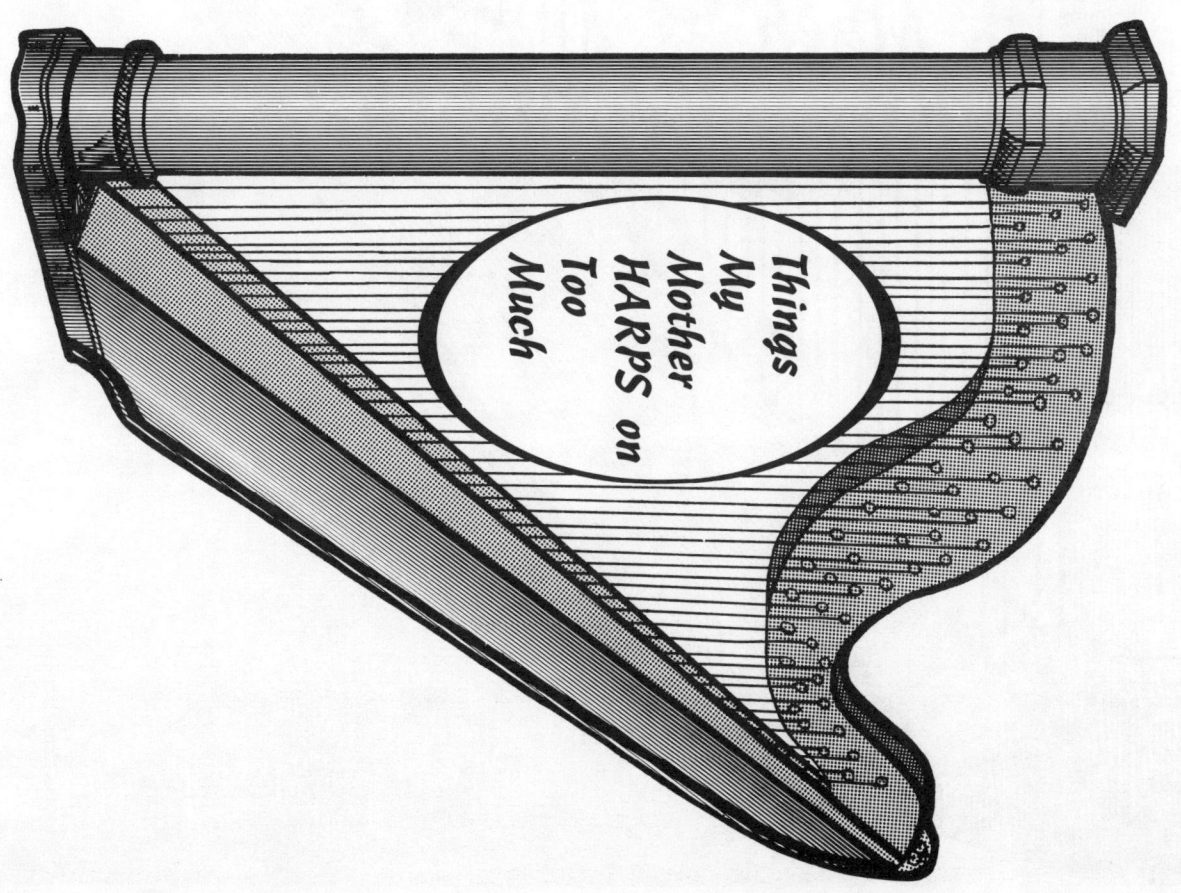

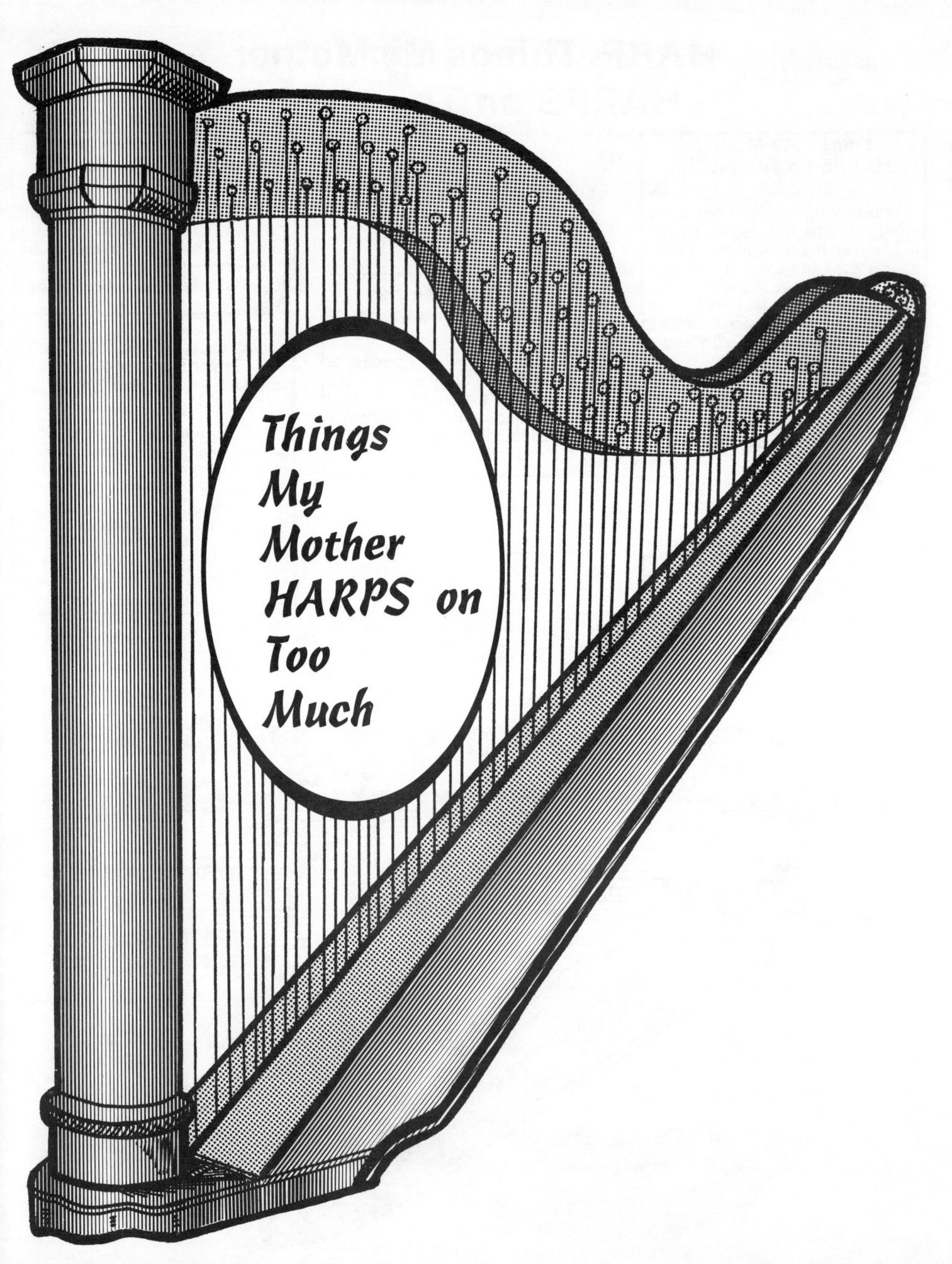

16: When I'm 16

When I'm 16
Story Starter

"But I've *never* had a birthday party," I complained to Mom.

"We'll give you one on your 16th birthday, and that's a promise," Mom answered.

"But that's such a long time off," I moaned.

"Then we'll let you plan it. You may have any kind of party you would like," she replied.

"Oh, boy! First I would like . . . ."

When I'm 16
Story Situation

Pretend that tomorrow will be your 16th birthday. You have waited for this day *forever.* You have been making plans for years. Tell about what will happen.

When I'm 16
Caption Substitutions

Sweet 16
16 Reasons Why . . . .
16 Reasons to Hug Your Mom
16 Candles
My Lucky Number

When I'm 16
Story Situation

You are traveling through a time machine until you reach your 16th birthday. You plan to stop for awhile and observe the differences in now and then. Relate *ten* differences that you feel are the most significant ones.

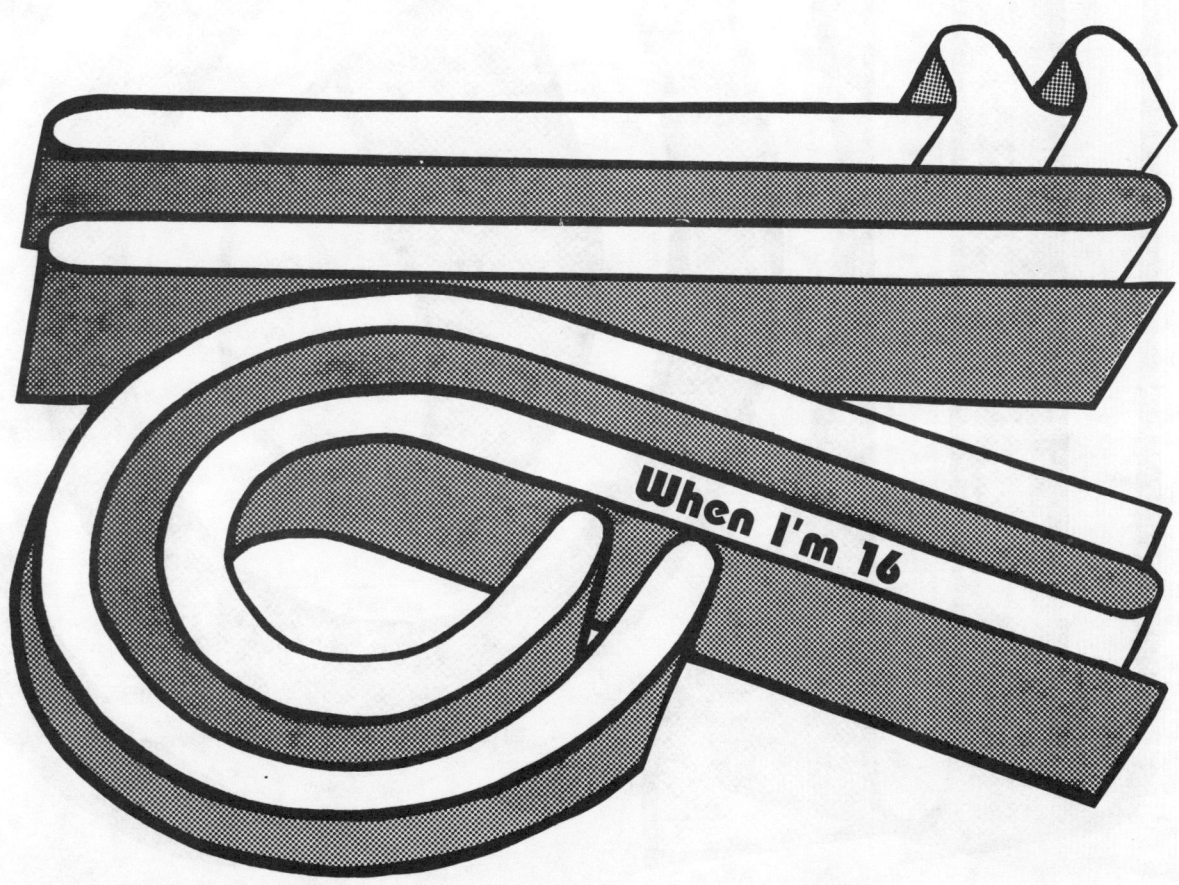

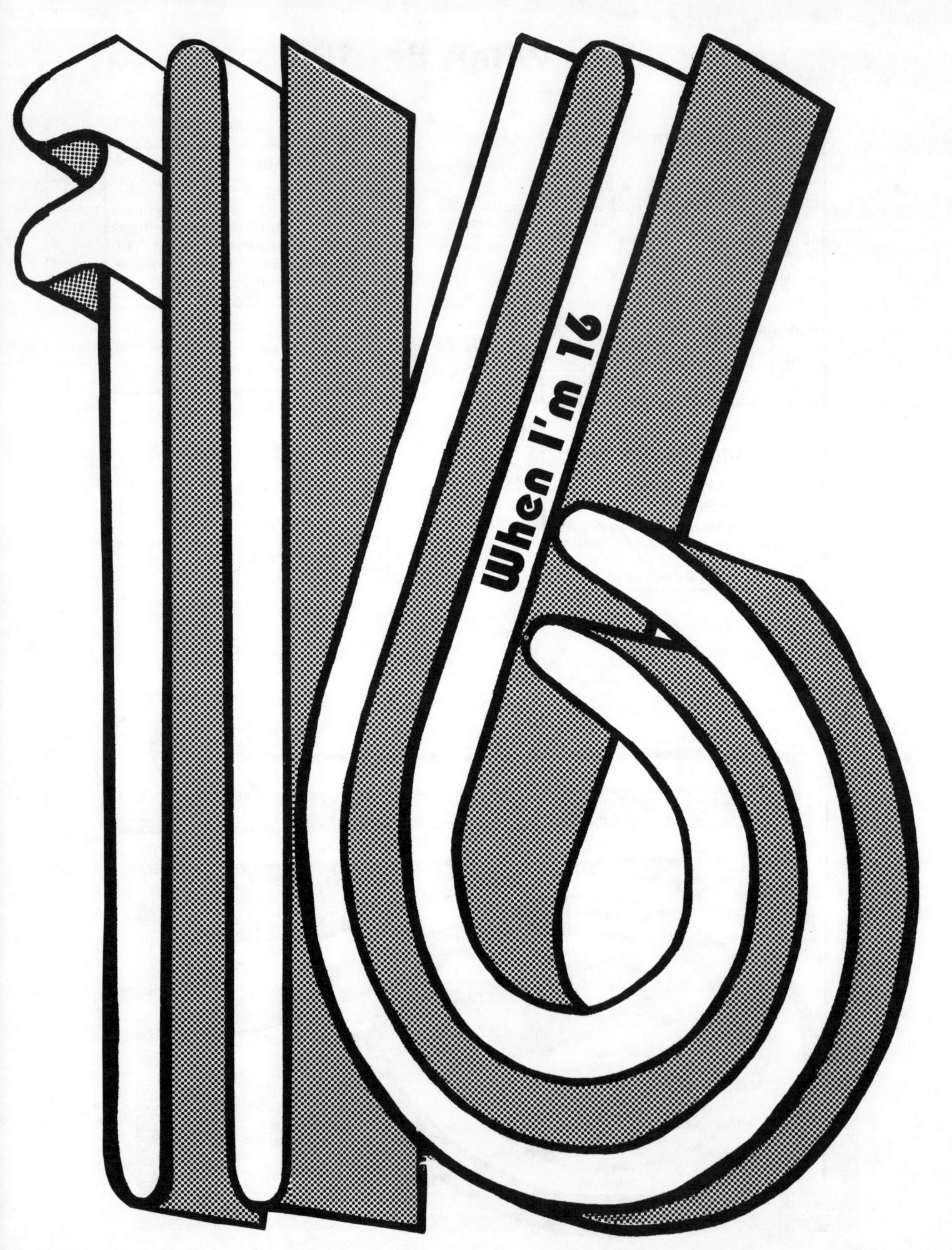

LIGHT SWITCH: Things That Turn Me Off

Things That Turn Me Off
Language Study

The expression "turn me off" generally refers to something unpleasant or something to be avoided. Think of several other expressions which might be used to describe things which we find unpleasant. Make a list of these expressions.

Things That Turn Me Off
Story Starter

At the top of the page was the word *off*.
"What are you writing?" I asked.
"I'm writing an essay on 'The World's Greatest Turnoffs,'" was the reply.
"Let me tell you what *I* think is the *one* greatest turnoff . . . ."

Things That Turn Me Off
Story Starter

The scene was one of terror. First came the shrill shattering of glass, then the dull thud. But neither of these prepared me for what followed . . . .

Things That Turn Me Off
Story Situation

Many things happen which "turn us off." Make a list of five things which turn *you* off. Tell *why* these actions are distasteful to you. Place a large check by the one you hate the most.

Things That Turn Me Off
Caption Substitutions

Things That Turn Me On
The Turning Point
A Switch in Time
A Shot in the Dark

Things That

Turn Me Off

CLOCK: Good Times

Good Times
Story Starter

Wow! This was the best time I ever had! I never knew I could have so much fun! Let me tell you about it . . . .

Good Times
Caption Substitutions

Once Upon a Time
A Timeless Story
Beat the Clock
The Time Machine
My Favorite Time of the Year
The Day Time Stood Still
The Day the Clocks Stopped
How Time Flies
It's About Time
No Time Like the Present
Just in Time

Good Times
Story Starter

We were supposed to have a great time. We *planned* to! We made all the necessary arrangements to do so. But then we suddenly looked up and . . . .

Good Times
Story Situation

Think of the *one* best time you have ever had. Describe it in detail. Tell who you were with, where you were, and all the things that helped you enjoy yourself.

Good Times
Decorative Possibilities

Instead of stationary hands on the clock, moveable hands may be attached. These may be attached at the center with a paper fastener and may actually be used in exercises with telling time with young children. Silver or gold self-adhesive decorative paper may be adhered to the trim of the clock.

BUG: Things That BUG Me

Things That BUG Me
Story Starter

"Don't Bug Me!"
"But I *don't* bug you. I'm really very nice to you!"
"No way! You irritate me constantly!"
"How?"
"Well, for starters . . . ."

Things That BUG Me
Language Study

The expression "that bugs me" refers to something which is found to be annoying, unpleasant, or aggravating. Make a list of some other expressions which are used when things are irritating. (Note that in the expression, the word *bug* does *not* refer to the insect. Words like *bug* which have different meanings in different contexts are called homographs.)

Things That BUG Me
Caption Substitutions

A Creepy Crawly Story
If I Were a Bug
My Volkswagen Bug
Small Crawly Things
The Buggy Ride
Snug as a Bug in a Rug

Things That BUG Me
Story Situation

Tomorrow is National Bug Day. Tell how you plan to celebrate it.

Things That BUG Me
Decorative Possibilities

Black or brown velveteen or felt fabrics may be glued onto the body shape of the bug. Moveable eyes may be used. Black or brown yarn may be glued onto the leg lines of the bug.

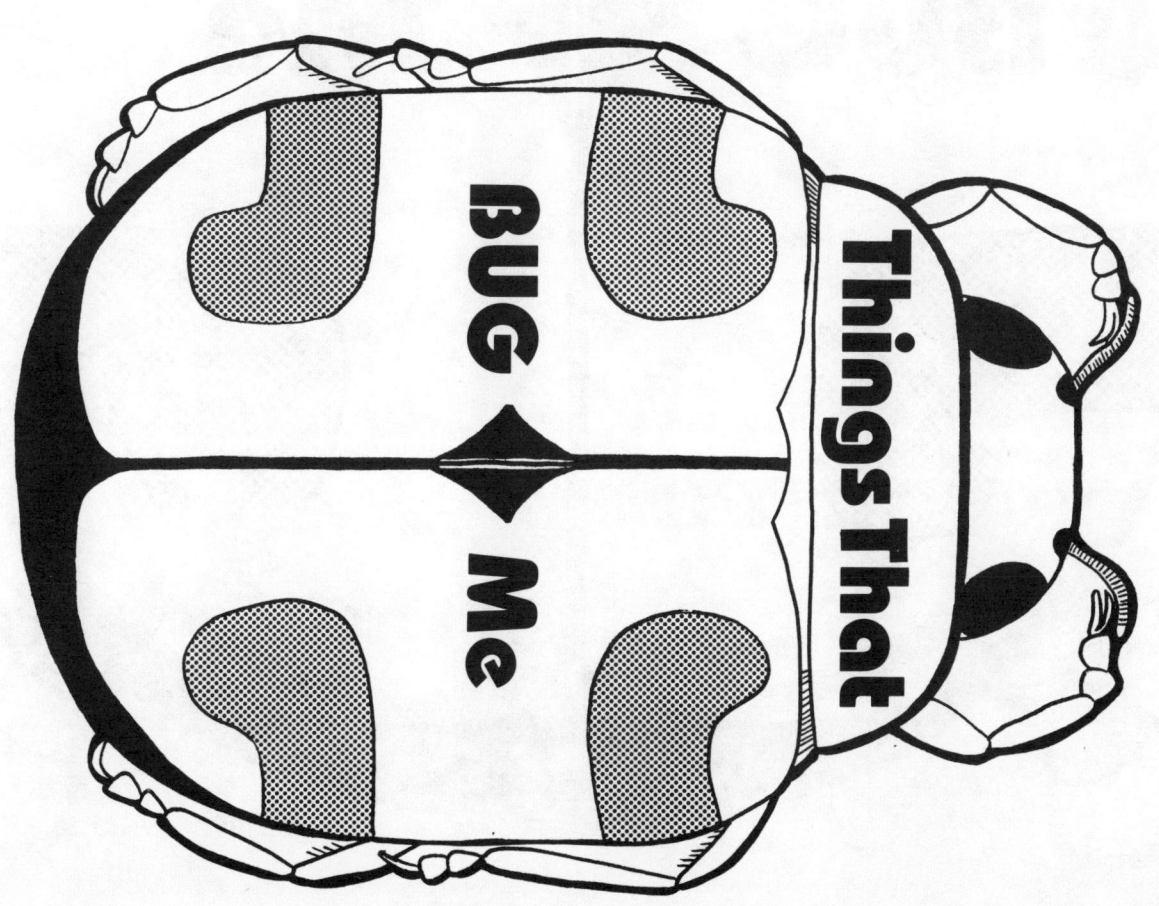

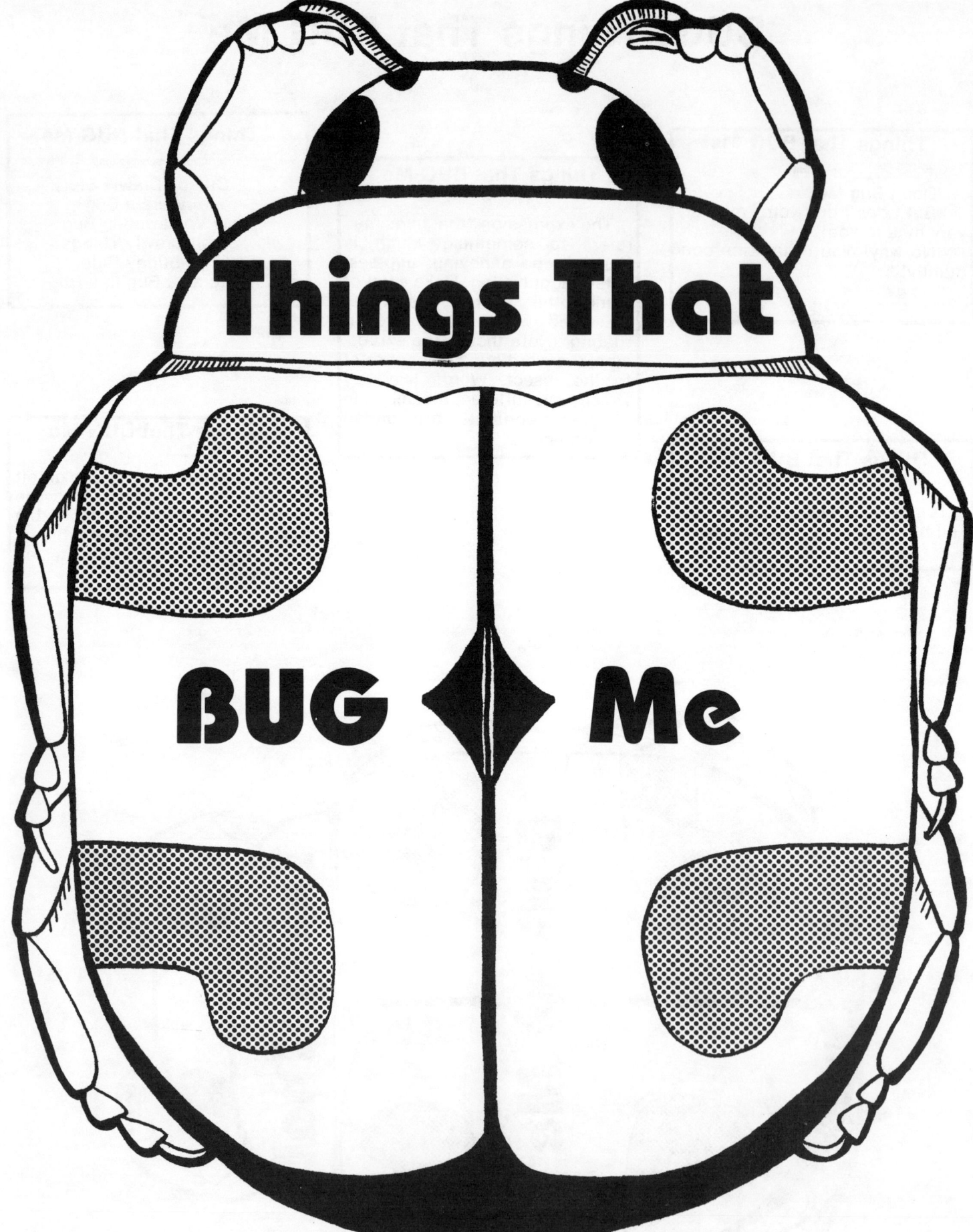

BANANA: An ApPEALing Tale

An ApPEALing Tale
Story Starter

A banana with sex appeal? Impossible! But that's what the man said. So, I bought one. On my way home . . . .

An ApPEALing Tale
Language Study

The second syllable in the word *appealing* is pronounced the same as the word *peel*. Since these two syllables have identical sounds, the phrase "appealing tale" might be used with the banana. Think of some other fruits which might be used with this same caption. Make a list of your choices.

An ApPEALing Tale
Decorative Possibilities

Cut the banana shape from yellow felt. Glue strings of black or brown yarn at the banana's definitive lines.

An ApPEALing Tale
Story Situation

Something terrific has just happened to you! It is so exciting that you have been asked to tell about it on *The Tonight Show*. Write the dialogue that will take place between you and the host of this show as you tell about this event.

An ApPEALing Tale
Caption Substitutions

The Banana That Split
Things That Drive Me Bananas
The Top Banana in My Life
I Go Bananas Over . . . .
When I Was as Hungry
  as a Gorilla
When It's Time to Split

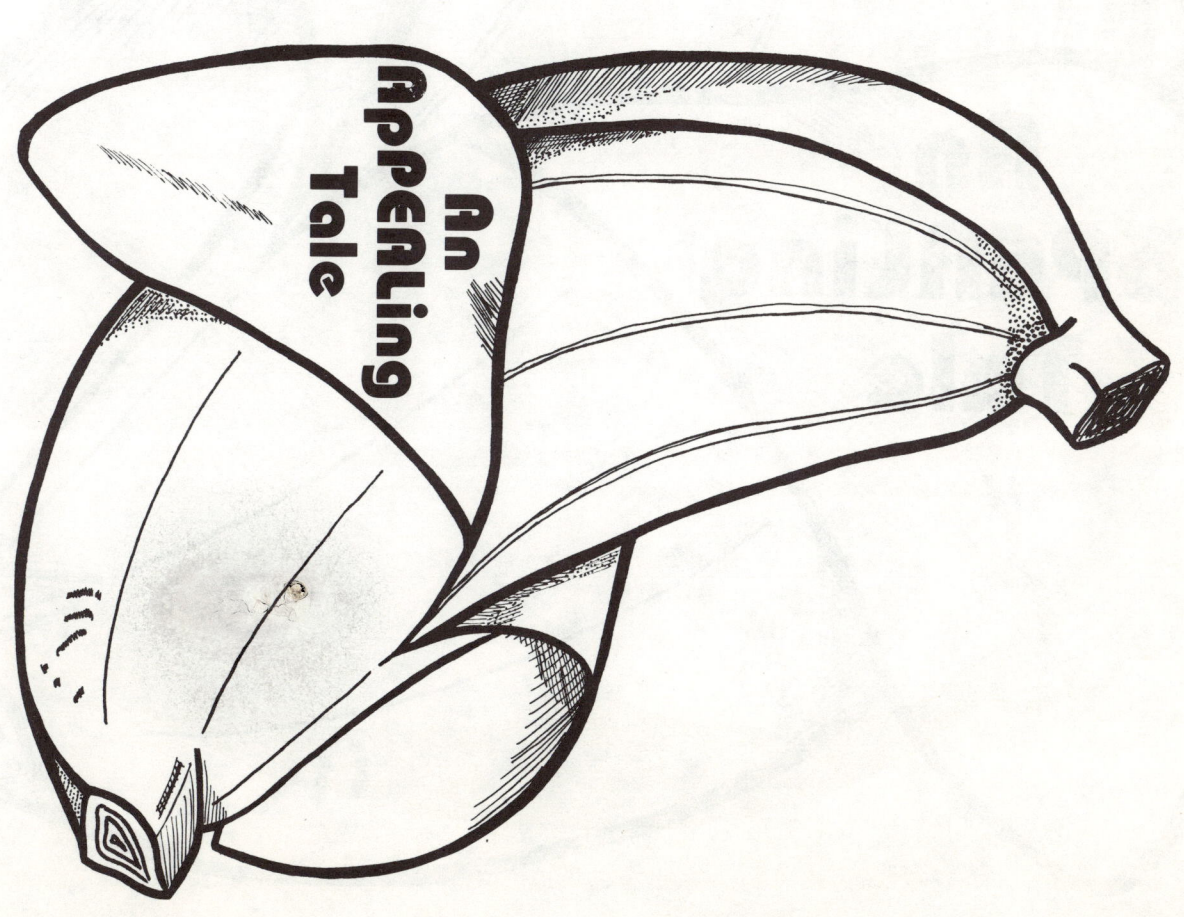

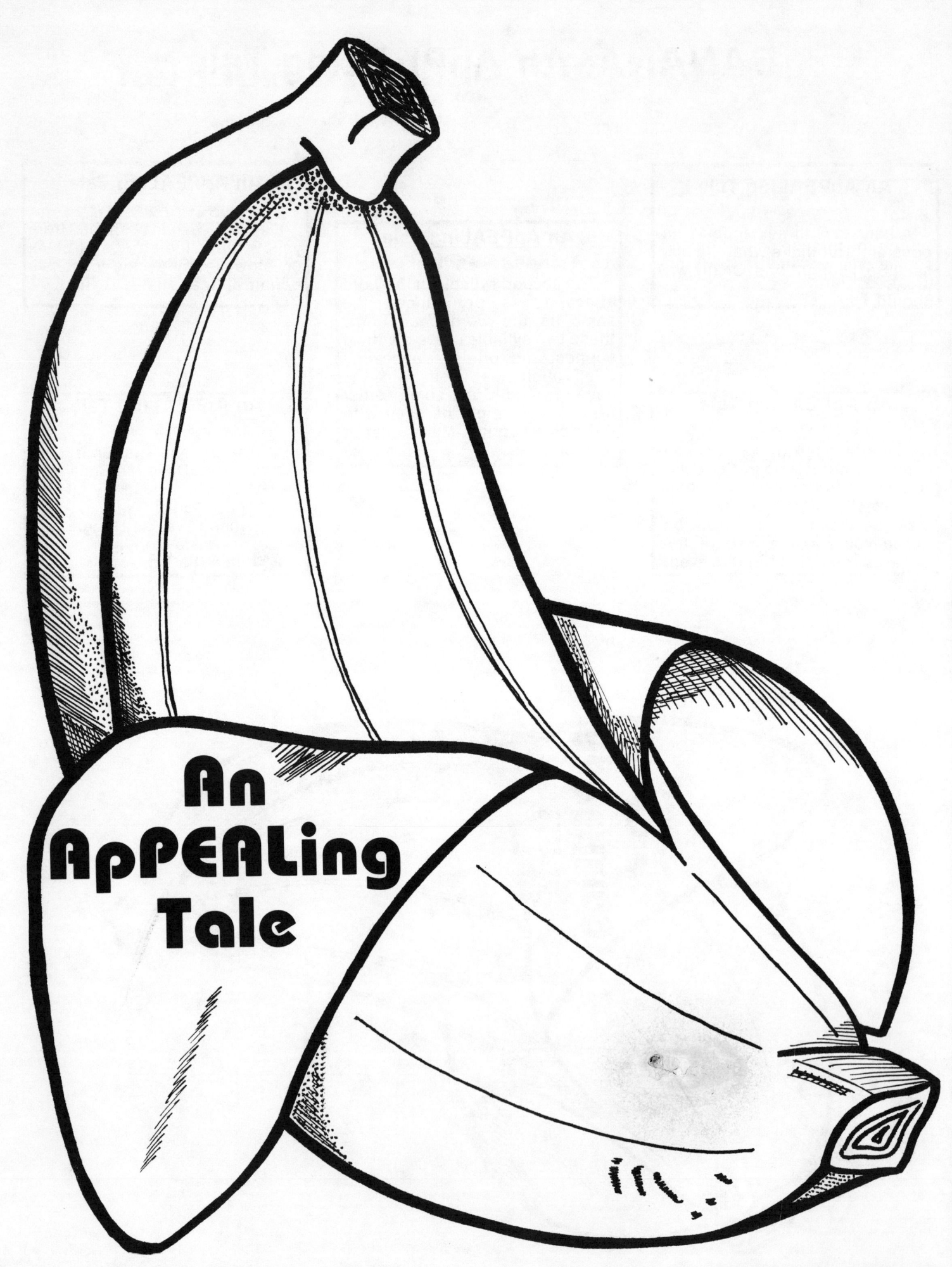

BOXING GLOVE: Things I'd Fight For

Things I'd Fight For
Story Starter
I felt the intense pain of his fist connecting with my jaw. My entire head throbbed from shock. Should I hit him back? I took a step in his direction . . . .

Things I'd Fight For
Story Situation
Although most people try to avoid actual "fights," there are things we all feel we would want to "fight for." Think about those things you feel very strongly about. Describe the *three* things that you would most want to defend if you felt they would be taken away from you without a "fight."

Things I'd Fight For
Decorative Possibilities
Leather fabric may be pasted onto a cardboard-shaped glove. Shoestrings or leather strips may add a special effect in the tied areas.

Things I'd Fight For
Story Starter
It was worth it! I am bruised and sore, but I feel better! It all started one morning when . . . .

Things I'd Fight For
Caption Substitutions
I'd Rather Fight Than Switch
PUNCH-U-8 These Sentences
Being PUNCH-ual
Punch and Judy
Times I've Been
Mad Enough to Fight
This Beats All!
Sock It to Me!

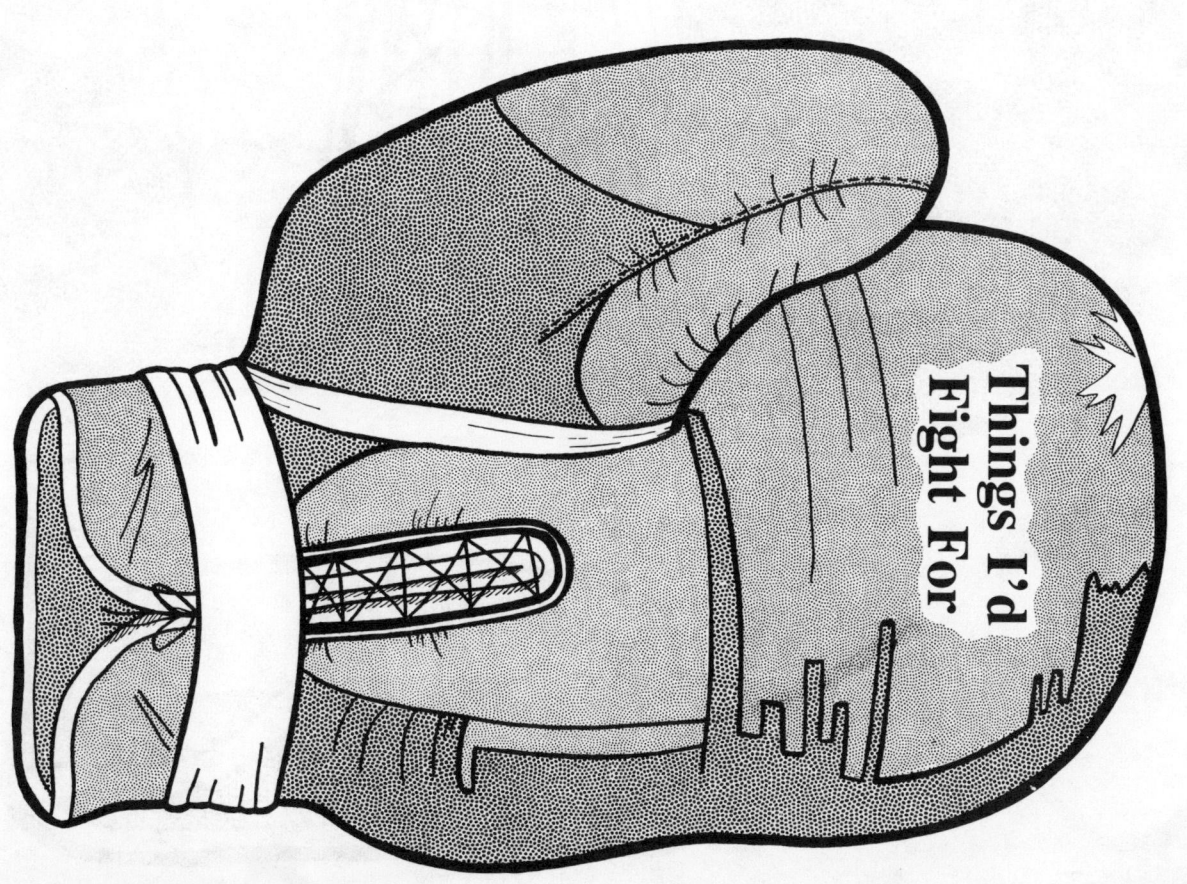

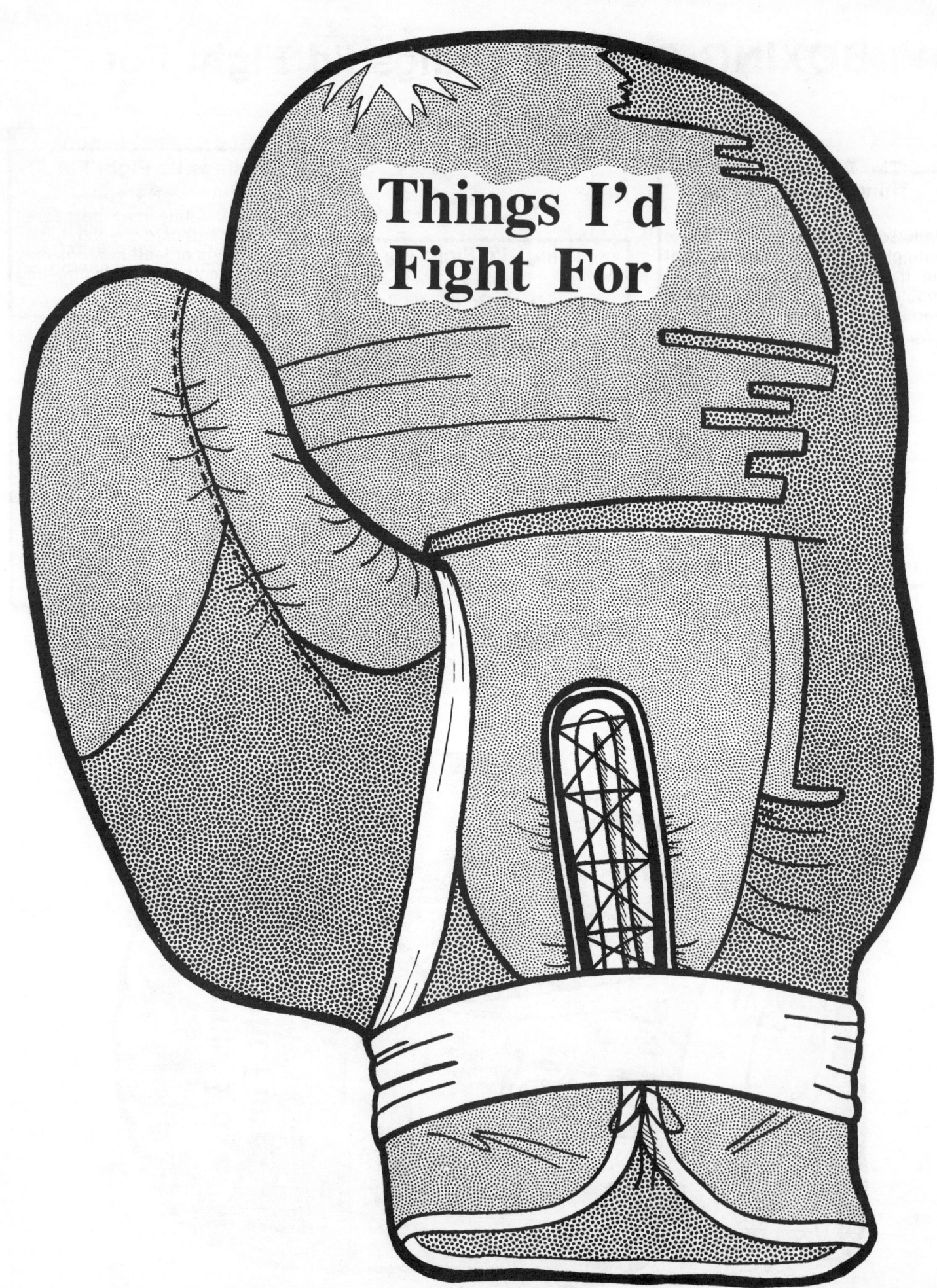

MATCH: The Perfect Match

The Perfect Match
Story Starter
There is one game I play really well. So far I have found no one who plays well enough to beat me. If I ever do, my opponent will be . . . .

The Perfect Match
Story Situation
You are engaged to be married. Your family has a tradition, however, that the oldest must marry first. You have one older sister who wears wigs made of steel wool, who causes little children to cry, who hangs upside down from the ceiling when she sleeps, and who always eats dead frogs for breakfast. She has never had a suitor and most men fight to keep away from her. However, you must find the "perfect match" for her before *you* will be allowed to marry. Tell how you plan to find her a husband.

The Perfect Match
Language Study
Homographs are words which are spelled the same but have different meanings. As used with this design, the word *match* is a homograph. One meaning of *match* is a short slender piece of wood tipped with a composition that can produce fire; another meaning is a person or thing that is equal to another.

The Perfect Match
Caption Substitutions
I'm No Match For . . . .
Things That Don't Match
Things I Find Striking
Getting Ahead
Two Heads Are Better Than One
My Matchless Friends

The Perfect Match
Decorative Possibilities
Glue light beige or red felt tips onto the match heads. For a two-dimensional effect, also glue strips of felt on the "top matches."

The Perfect Match

BOWLING PINS: Things That BOWL Me Over

Things That BOWL Me Over
Story Starter
Yesterday my older sister came home and announced that she was planning to marry. However, the one she plans to marry is a Martian. This news really bowled me over. In fact, I can think of only one other thing that has ever shocked me more. That was the time when . . . .

Things That BOWL Me Over
Story Situation
At the end of the alley are ten pins which you need to knock over. However, there are no bowling balls or other round heavy objects for you to use. You must stand at the usual bowler's position. You will have your choice of any two objects that are not round. Decide what these two objects will be and tell how you plan to knock over the pins without walking closer to them.

Things That BOWL Me Over
Language Study
The expression "bowl me over" is used to refer to those things which overwhelm us with surprise. What other expressions do you use in reference to that which you find overwhelming? Make a list of these expressions.

Things That BOWL Me Over
Caption Substitutions
What I'd Hate to Meet in an Alley
Times I've Felt Pinned Down
The Pinnacle of Success

Things That BOWL Me Over
Decorative Possibilities
A wood-grain self-adhesive paper may be placed atop the drawn design of the pins.

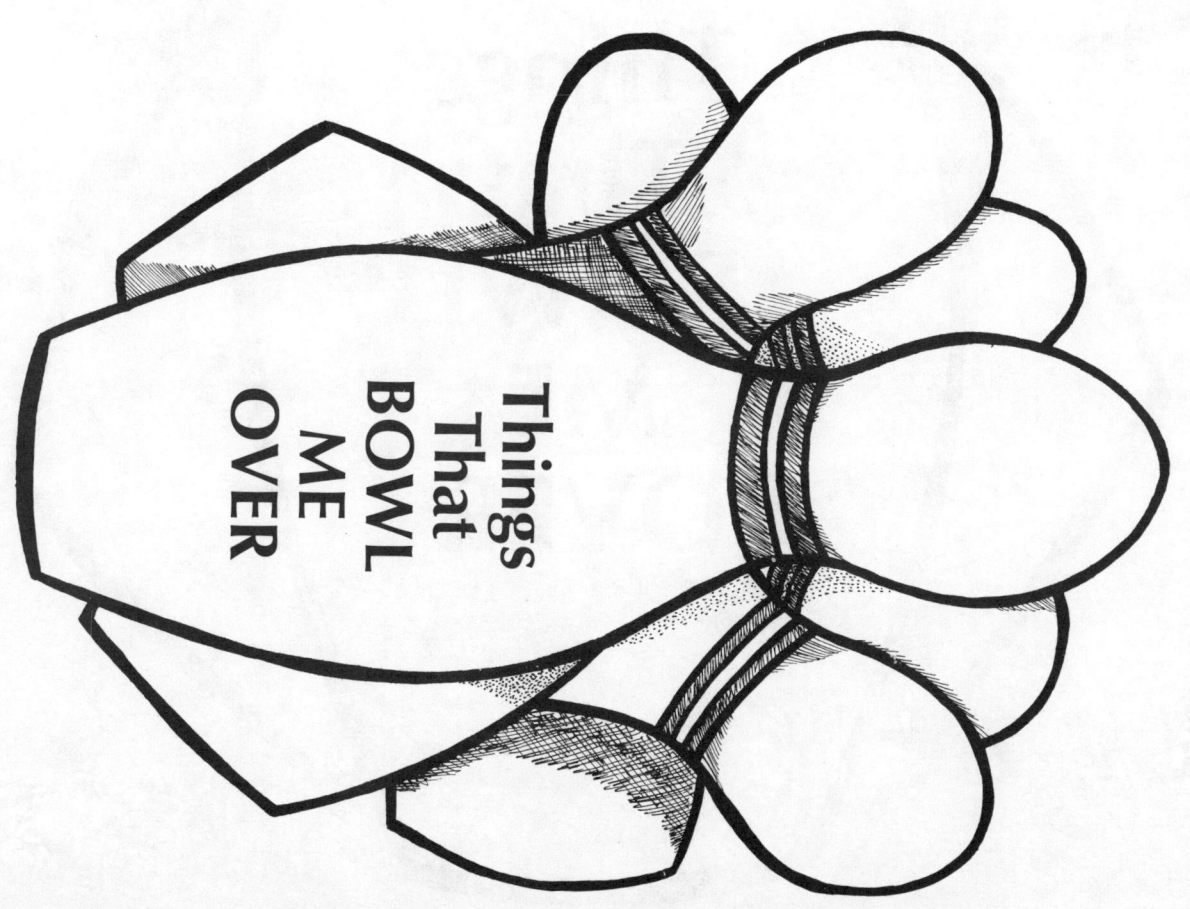

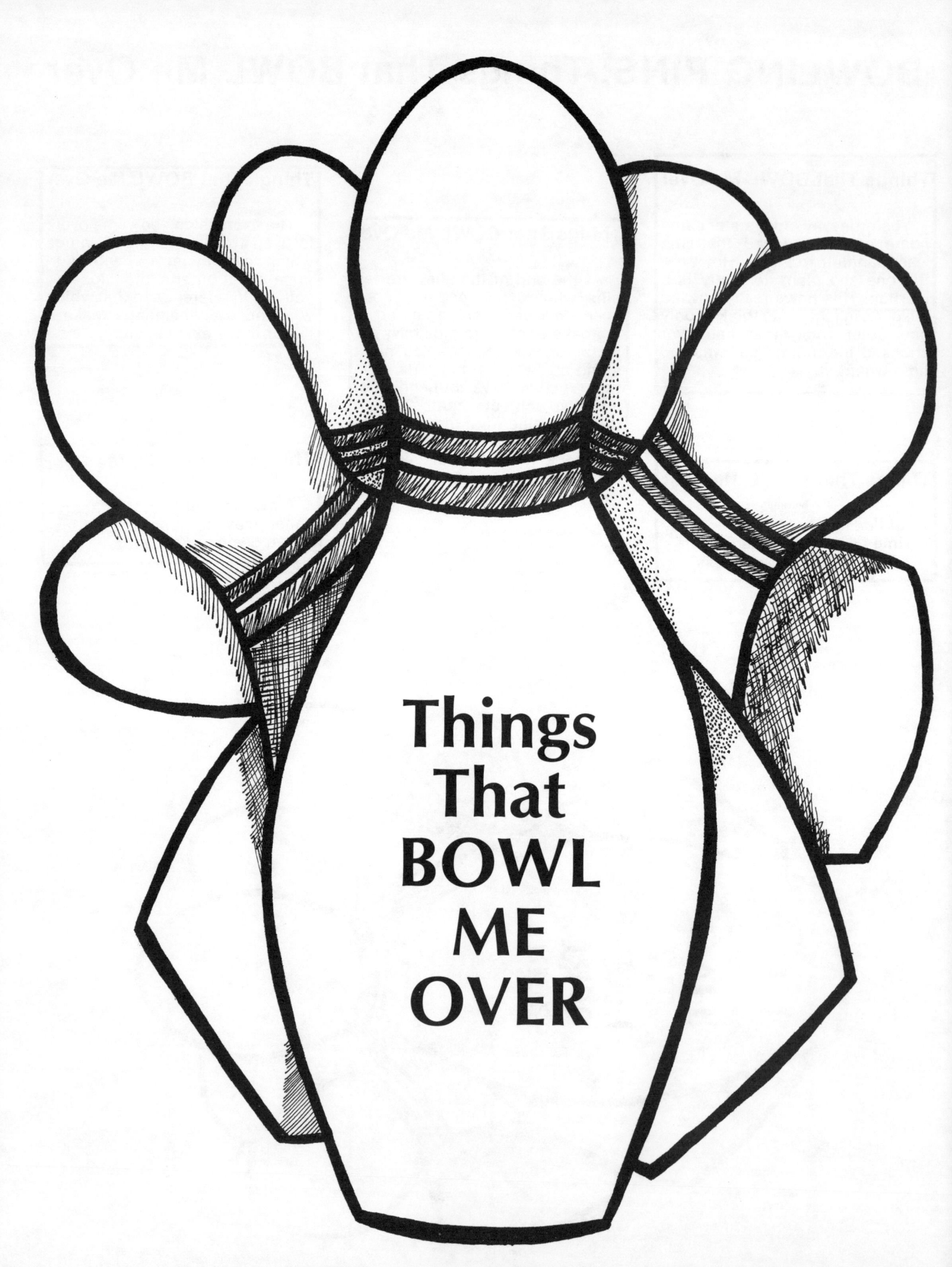

CHEST: My Treasures

My Treasures
Story Starters

Many things are of great value to me. There are many things I would hate to give up. But the one thing I treasure MOST of all is....

My Treasures
Story Starter

Hidden deep in my closet is a chest filled with treasures I have collected for many years. This chest is filled with some of the most unique and fascinating items known to man. One of these items....

My Treasures
Decorative Possibilities

Gold foil may be wrapped around circular pieces of oaktag paper and glued into the center of the chest. Wood-grain or silver self-adhesive paper may be used for the outside of the chest area.

My Treasures
Caption Substitutions

If I Had a Million Dollars
Things of Value to Me
Getting Things Off My Chest
Times I Treasure
People I Treasure
My Hope Chest

My Treasures
Story Starter

Some of my most prized treasures are my memories of pleasurable experiences I have had. The one greatest memory was the time when....

HAT: Keep This Under Your Hat

Keep This Under Your Hat
Story Starter

A small squirrel scampered through the meadow. She heard the warning thunder and felt a drop of rain. What would she do with her newfound treasure during the storm? She looked all around. No shelter was in sight. Then she spied a hat that seemed to have been left behind. She crept closer . . . .

Keep This Under Your Hat
Story Situation

Sometimes we tell our friends or family members something we don't ever want them to tell anyone else. We tell them to "keep it under their hat" or to keep it a secret. However, the secret is not always kept. At times this can cause pain or embarrassment for you or others involved. Tell about one time when a secret was not kept and you felt hurt or embarrassed.

Keep This Under Your Hat
Caption Substitutions

Hat Tricks
I Get Mad as a Hatter When . . . .
My Trip to ManHATtan
The Hat Left on the Murder Scene
The Case of the Missing Hat
Hats Off To . . . .
Can You Top This?
Things I'm on Top Of!

Keep This Under Your Hat
Language Study

The expression "keep this under your hat" is a request for the given information to be kept secret. If you have a secret which you don't want a friend to share with anyone, how would you make this request? List some phrases which you might use.

Keep This Under Your Hat
Decorative Possibilities

Various types of fabric, especially felt, velveteen, and ribbon, may be glued onto cardboard and cut into this hat design. A velveteen hat band, for example, can add a very special effect. Hats may also be any color or color combinations.

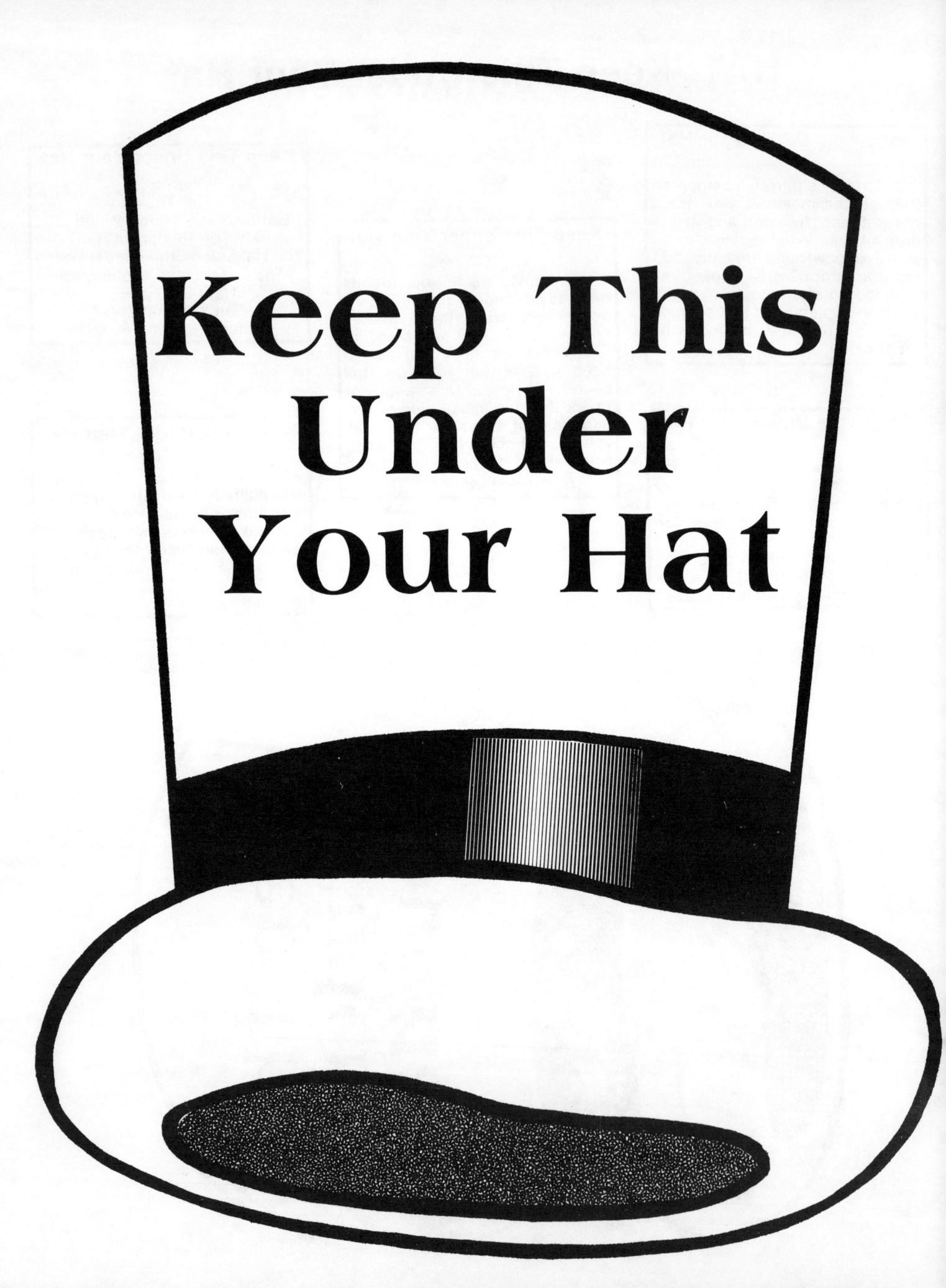

FAN: A FANtastic Person

A FANtastic Person
Story Situation
Think about all of the fantastic people you have met or know about through the news media. Which one person impresses you the most? Name this person and tell why you feel he or she is fantastic.

A FANtastic Person
Caption Substitutions
My Favorite FANtasy
I'm a FAN-atic About . . . .
A "FAN-C" Story
Without Much FANfare
My FAN Club
FANtastic Finishes
The Egg Really Hit the Fan When . . . .

(Any other words with the letter sequence *f-a-n* may be used in a clever title.)

A FANtastic Person
Language Study
In the word *fantastic,* the first syllable is sometimes over-stressed, possibly causing one to think of a real fan. This type of play on words may help create clever titles for stories. List other words with the letter sequence *f-a-n* which could be used in clever titles for this design. Write these titles.

A FANtastic Person
Story Starter
The old man ambled down the sidewalk. Few people would ever know about the good deed he had just performed. He did not wait for a reward or even for thanks. But I saw what he did and I want to tell about it . . . .

A FANtastic Person
Decorative Possibilities
Aluminum foil or silver self-adhesive paper may be used on metal fan parts. Glitter may also be used in these places. Strings, yarn, rubber bands, or thin wires may be glued on as the wires in the blade guard.

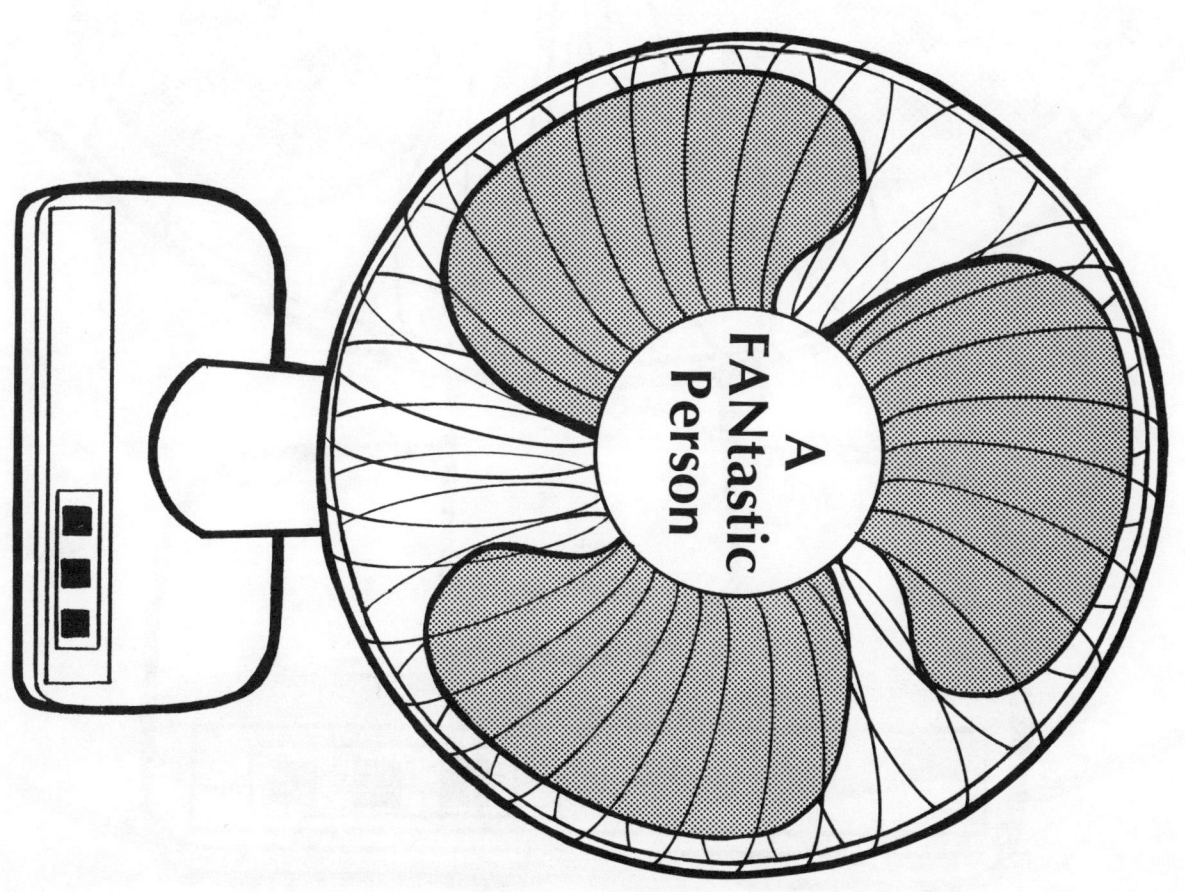

DINOSAUR: Things I Wish Were Extinct

Things I Wish Were Extinct
Story Situation
You have suddenly been given a special magic power. Anything will disappear if you say the magic words. However, *all* things in that category will disappear (not just one particular one), and they will *never* return. Make a list of all of these things which you would like to become extinct.

Things I Wish Were Extinct
Caption Substitution
What Made Dinah Sore?

Things I Wish Were Extinct
Story Situation
The meeting of the "Children's Concerns Club" had just adjourned. One law was passed in this meeting. It read, "From this day forth, there will be *no little brothers* allowed in any home." All the children at this meeting were happy with this law. All voted for it to pass.

Twenty years have gone by. Describe some problems you think might have occurred by now if every family obeyed this law after it was passed.

Things I Wish Were Extinct
Language Study
The word *extinct* means no longer living or active. The pictured dinosaur is an example of an extinct animal. Make a list of other things that might be classified as extinct. Remember that these items may be either animals or inactive things.

Things I Wish Were Extinct
Decorative Possibilities
Movable eyes may be used at the corresponding place on the dinosaur design.

2: It Hurts TOO Much

It Hurts TOO Much
Story Starter
When I have a really bad nightmare, I am always dreaming that someone is giving me a shot. Sometimes it is a flu shot, sometimes an allergy shot, and sometimes *many* shots for different reasons. Today my mom made me go to the doctor. They ran some tests and then told me . . . .

It Hurts TOO Much
Language Study
Words which sound the same but have different spellings and meanings are called homophones. The words *too, two,* and *to* are examples. *Two* means one plus one. *Too* means also. *To* is a preposition having many functional uses but generally meaning in the direction toward. Write one sentence in which all three of these homophones could be used. (One example might be: "It was *too* late for Jim *to* buy *two* tickets.")

It Hurts TOO Much
Caption Substitutions
When I Was TWO
TOO Many Times I . . . .
TOO Little, TOO Late
I Ate TOO Much When . . . .
Things That Occur in TWO's
TOday
Things That Belong 2-gether

It Hurts TOO Much
Story Starter
I simply *can't* stand up in front of my class and read my report. My teacher just doesn't understand how much it hurts to do that. I must devise a plan . . . .

DOG: A DOGgone Good Story

A DOGgone Good Story
Story Starter

It was my turn next. All of the other contestants had been eliminated except the two of us. Butterflies filled my stomach. Waves of courage came and left in fluctuating cycles. I stepped up on the stage . . . .

A DOGgone Good Story
Language Study

The expression "doggone" generally refers to something we do not like very well. The word or forms of the word *dog* appear in several expressions which we use. Make a list of as many expressions containing a form of the word *dog* as you can.

A DOGgone Good Story
Caption Substitutions

It's a Dog's Life
Doggone It!
A Dogged Individual
A Dog I'd Like to Have
Dog Days

A DOGgone Good Story
Story Starter

Dear Diary: A really good thing happened to me today. I must tell you about it. For the *first* time in my life . . . .

A DOGgone Good Story
Decorative Possibilities

Fake-fur may be glued onto a piece of cardboard shaped like the dog design. A moveable eye may be glued onto the appropriate place. Red felt may be used for the tongue.

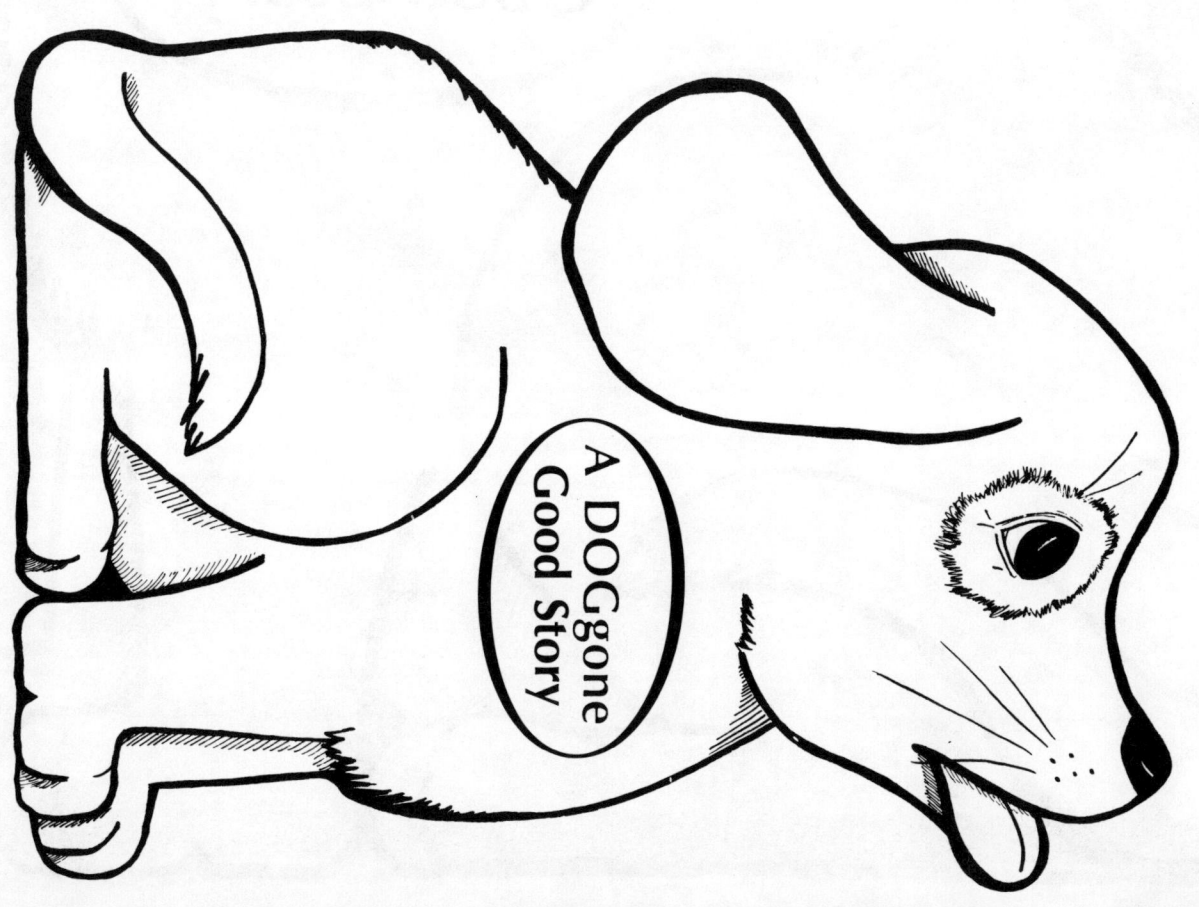

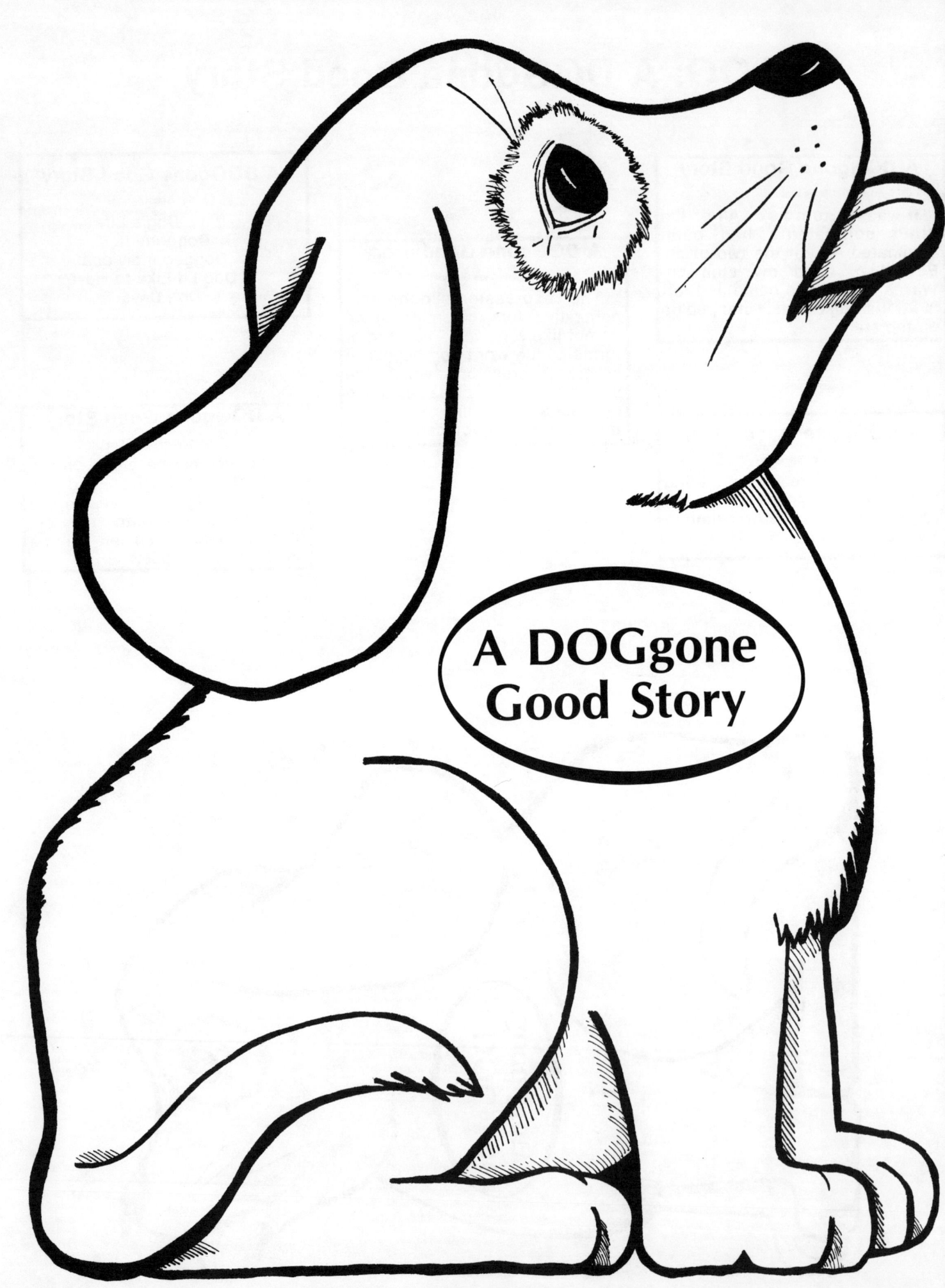

NO

NO
Story Situation
You are having a serious argument which involves every member of your family. They all want you to go with them to visit Aunt Matilda, but you want to stay at home. The conversation is getting heated. You really don't want to go. Write a short conversation which might reflect this argument. However, this conversation is one in which the word *no* cannot be used.

NO
Story Situation
Make a list of all the negative phrases you have heard during the last week. Place a check by the ones you hope you will never hear again.

NO
Story Situation
"Mr. No" is a person with very special powers. You may ask him as many questions as you wish. His answers to *all* of these questions will always be "No." These situations will then immediately become reality. For example, if you ask him, "Will I pass my test tomorrow?" he will say "No." At that point, there will be no way you will ever be able to pass the test. However, if you had asked, "Will I score below 95 on my test tomorrow?" his answer will still be "No," and you would make a score of at least 96.

Make a list of 20 questions you would like to ask Mr. No.

NO
Story Situation
From now on you are only allowed to say "no" *one* time each week. Tell one way you think your life will change because of this.

NO
Caption Substitutions
No caption is printed onto the design for "NO." One *may* be written, however, if desired. The following may be considered:

My Favorite Word
My Little Brother's Favorite Word
NO Way!
A Word My Mom Hates to Hear
A Word I Use Too Frequently
Oh, NO!
A Scream in the Night
I Want NO Part Of . . . .

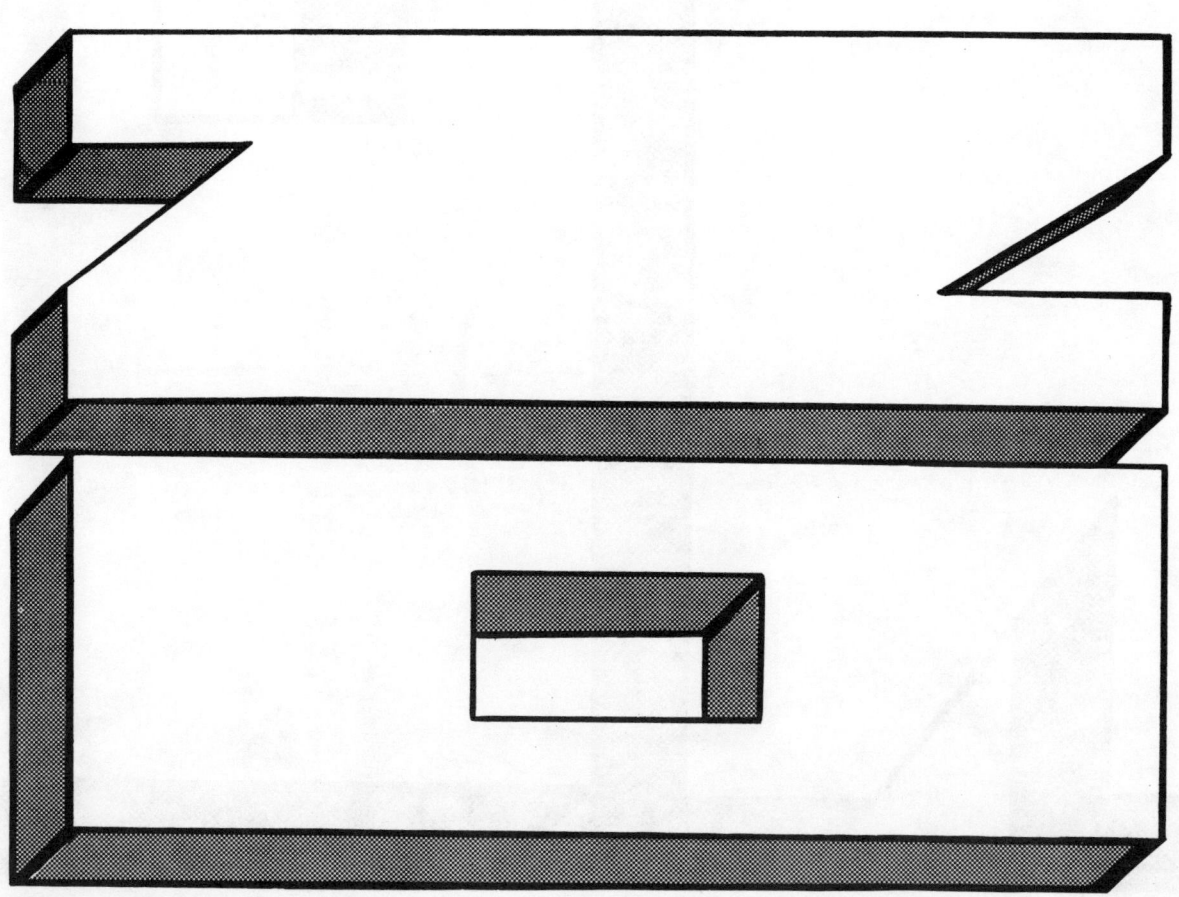

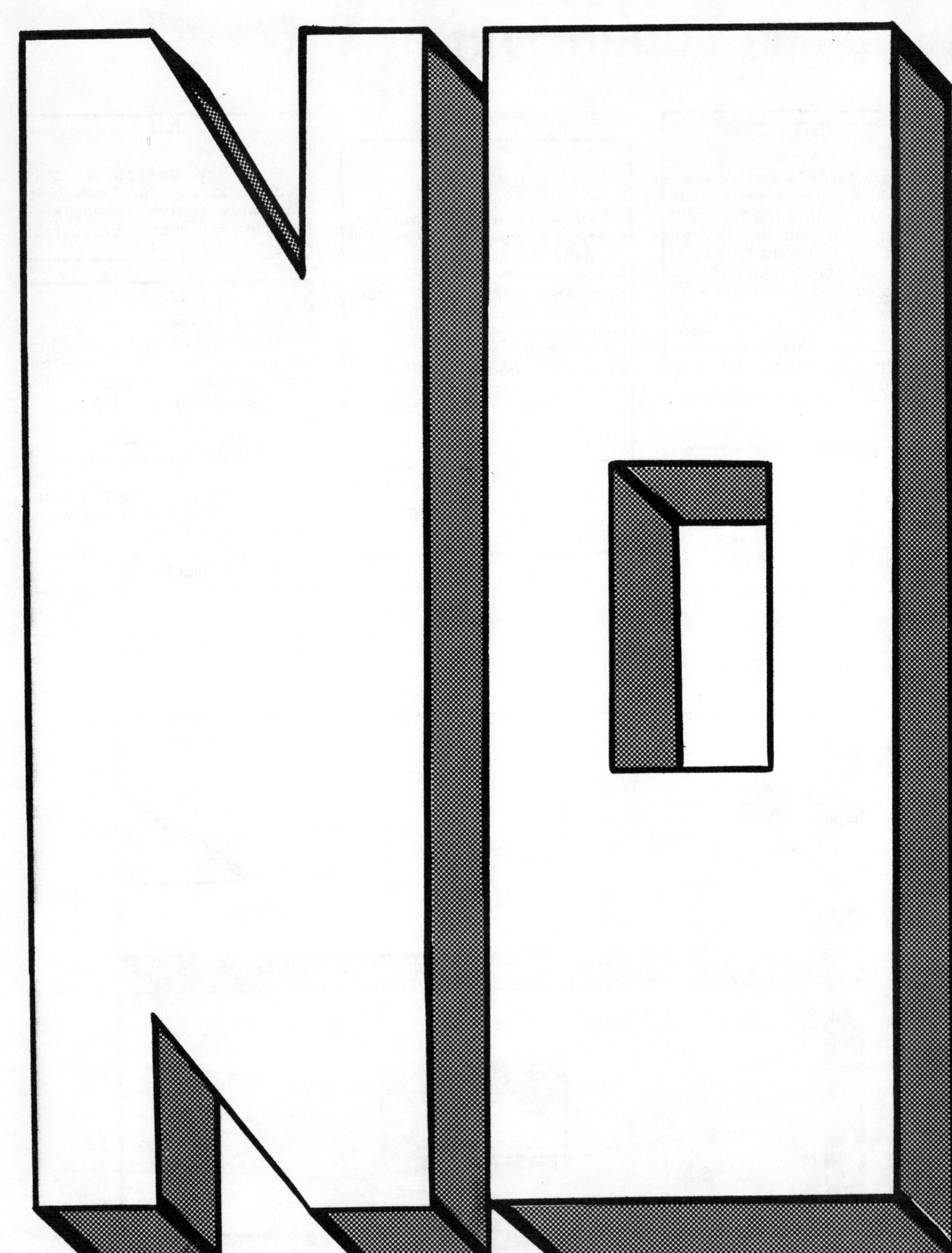

CORN: A Corny Story

A Corny Story
Story Starter

Once upon a time my little brother brought a purple turtle home with him. This turtle was quite unusual because it would grow horns whenever we played country music. It would flip its shell in the air whenever my brother whistled. But that's not even the best part . . . .

A Corny Story
Story Situation

The Corny Story Contest is on! You know you will win because you can tell about the time. . . .

A Corny Story
Language Study

The word *corn* has many meanings. One meaning refers to the yellow vegetable which may be eaten in various fashions. The word *corny* generally refers to trite or tiresomely simple sayings. What other expressions are used in these cases?

A Corny Story
Story Starter

That is the corniest thing I have ever heard! I just can't believe he expects me to fall for this! Here is what he told me . . . .

A Corny Story
Caption Substitutions

Lend Me Your EAR
Oh, SHUCKS
My Promotion to KERNEL
A Kiss Behind the EAR

A Corny Story
Decorative Possibilities

At the appropriate time of the year, a real (or dried) corn shuck may be glued onto the outside of the corn design.

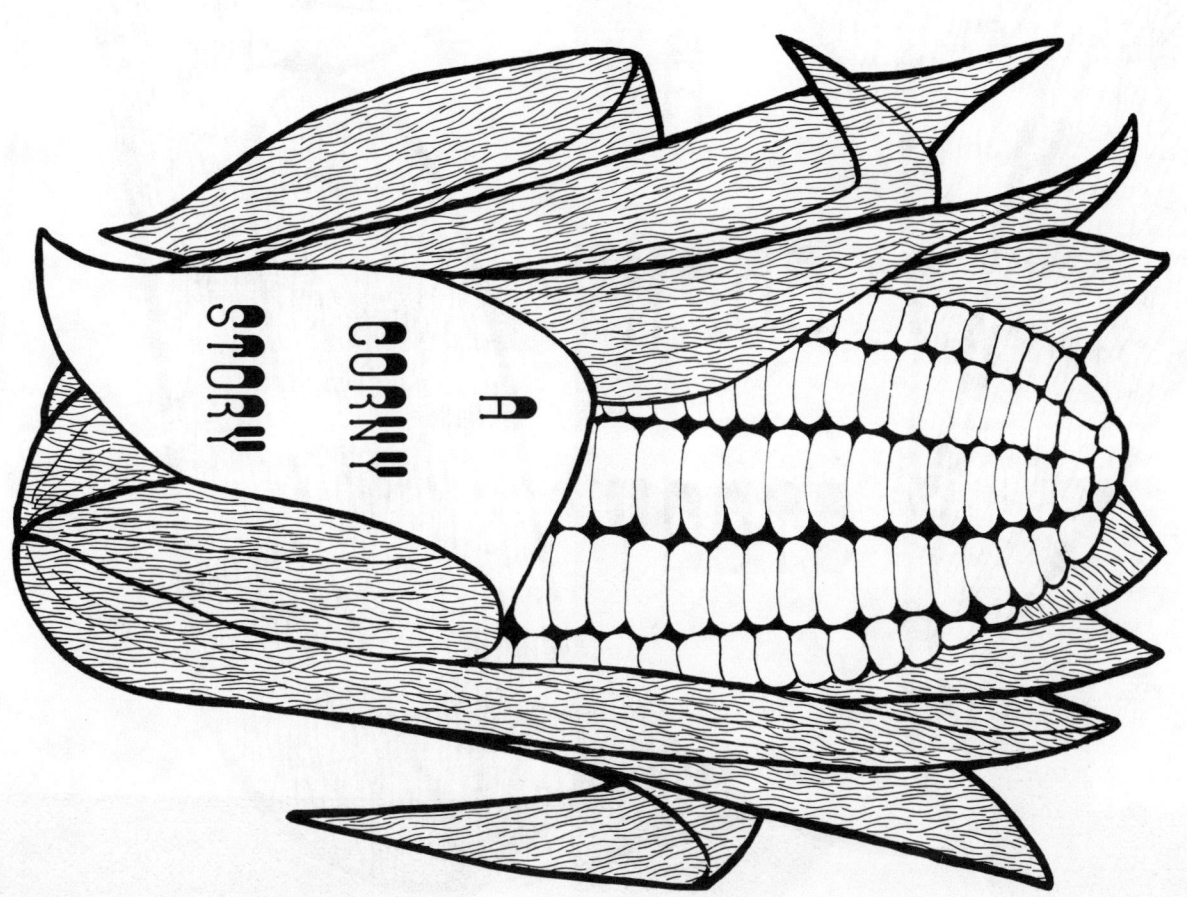

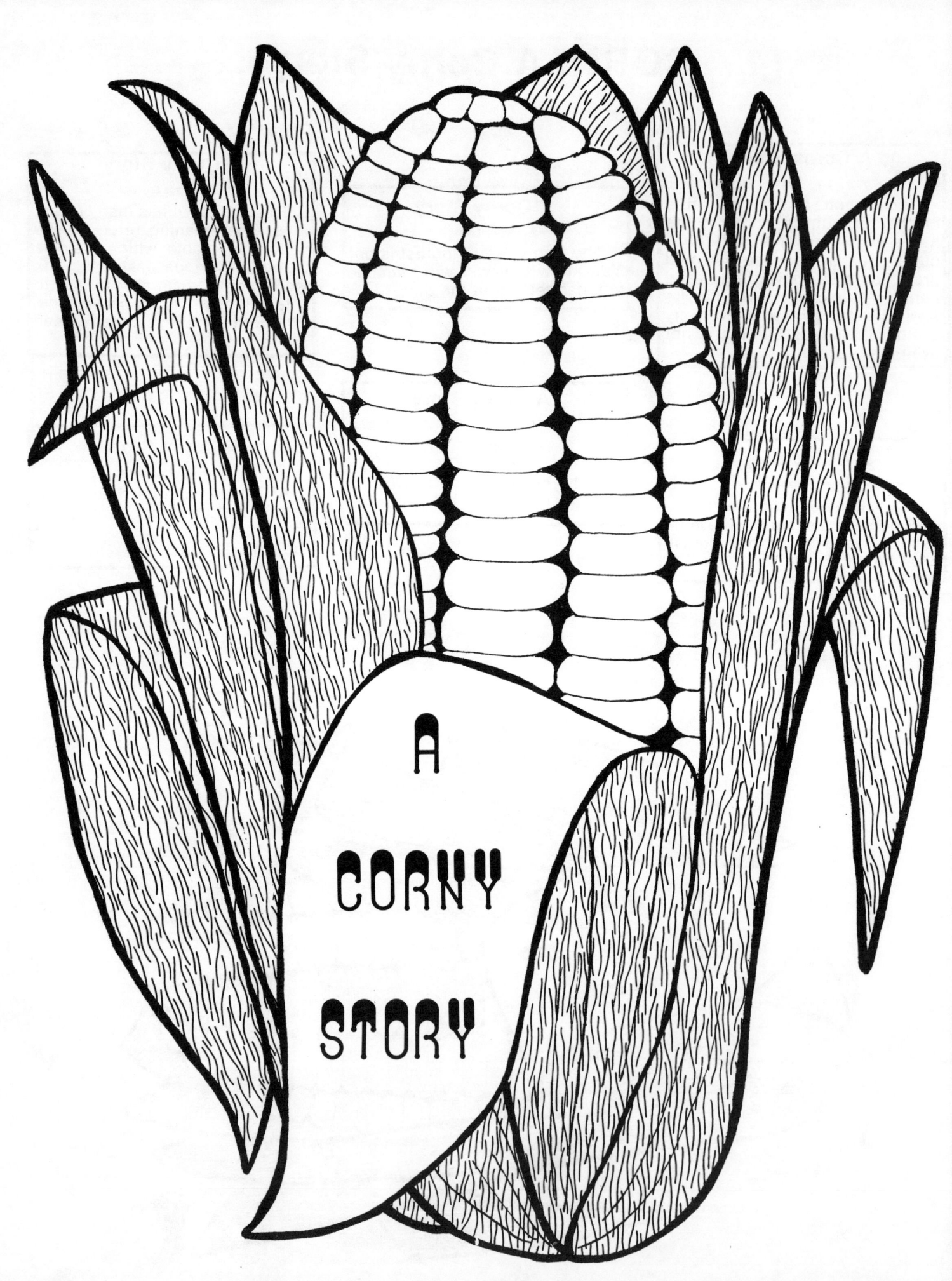

BALLOON: An Uplifting Experience

An Uplifting Experience
Story Situation
You have just won a two-week vacation in Hawaii for you and your best friend. The only problem is that you must agree to be transported in a large balloon. You have never traveled in such a vehicle and you are not sure how you will like it. Pretend you are on your way there now and describe your feelings concerning this "flight."

An Uplifting Experience
Story Starter
Our team was having a losing streak. Two of our best players were away on a trip. I was substituting for one of them. It was my turn next at bat . . . .

An Uplifting Experience
Story Situation
Have you ever suddenly felt uplifted when a friend or acquaintance gave you a nice genuine compliment? Write five compliments which you would really like to hear someone sincerely give you. Select *one* of these five and outline a course of action so this compliment could eventually be a sincere one.

An Uplifting Experience
Caption Substitutions
Things Full of Hot Air
Competition for the Airlines
Things to Do on a Hot Afternoon
A Hot Air Story
Things That Make Me Feel High

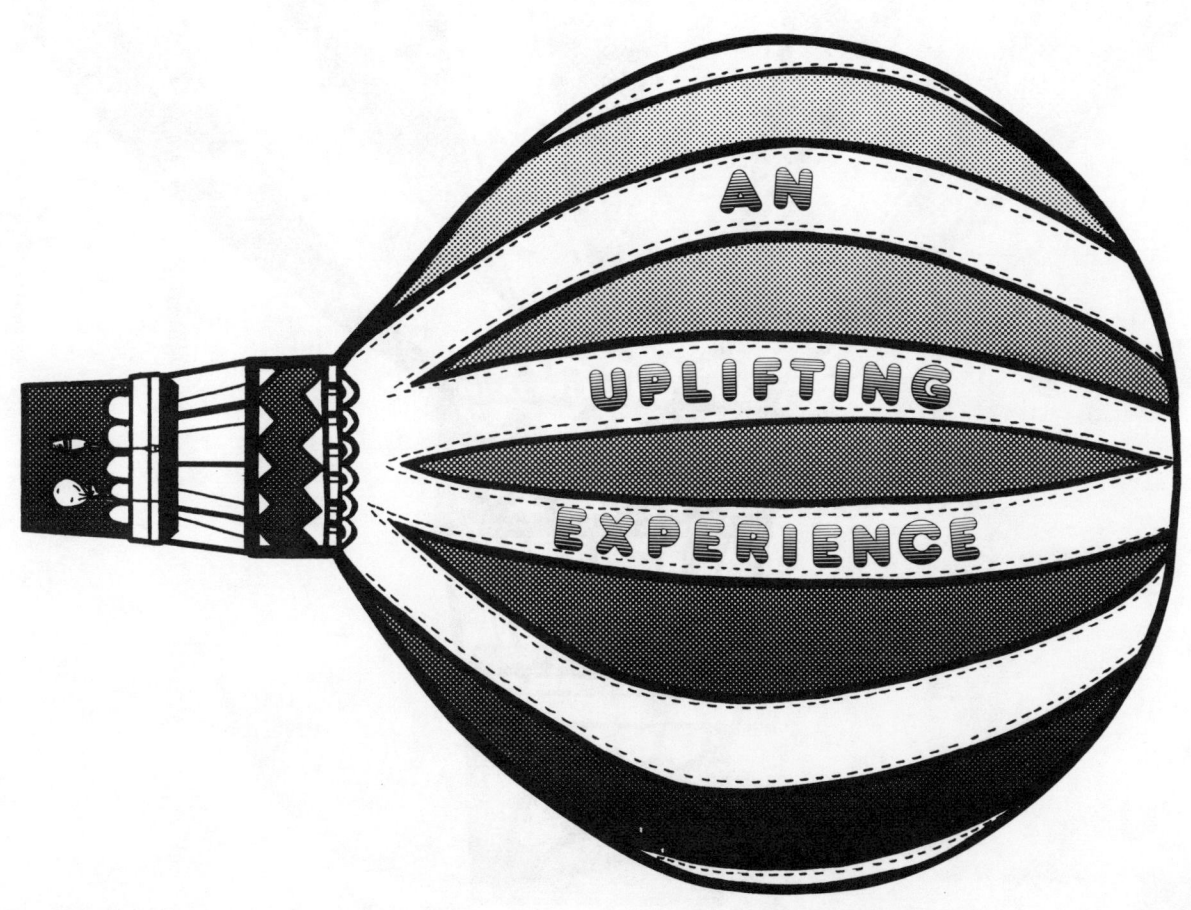